MEDIEVAL *ARTES PRAEDICANDI*: A SYNTHESIS OF SCHOLASTIC SERMON STRUCTURE

Medieval Academy Books, No. 114

SIEGFRIED WENZEL

Medieval *Artes Praedicandi*: A Synthesis of Scholastic Sermon Structure

Published for The Medieval Academy of America by
University of Toronto Press 2015

University of Toronto Press
Toronto Buffalo London
www.utppublishing.com

ISBN 978-1-4426-5010-7

Library and Archives Canada Cataloguing in Publication

Wenzel, Siegfried, 1928–, author
Medieval artes praedicandi : a synthesis of scholastic sermon structure / Siegfried Wenzel.

(Medieval Academy books ; no. 114)
Includes bibliographical references and index.
ISBN 978-1-4426-5010-7 (bound)

1. Sermons, Medieval – History and criticism. 2. Rhetoric, Medieval. 3. Preaching – Study and teaching – History – Middle Ages, 600–1500. I. Title. II. Series: Medieval Academy books ; no. 114

BV4207.W35 2015 251.009'02 C2014-907822-6

University of Toronto Press acknowledges the financial assistance to its publishing program of the Canada Council for the Arts and the Ontario Arts Council, an agency of the Government of Ontario.

University of Toronto Press acknowledges the financial support of the Government of Canada through the Canada Book Fund for its publishing activities.

Contents

Part IV: Other Issues

Acknowledgments

In studying medieval treatises on sermon structure I have been much helped by long years of reading medieval sermons and reflecting on their designs. For being able to do this, I thank the librarians and staff of many libraries in England and the Continent, whose holdings I was allowed to see and of which I often could acquire microfilms and scanned reproductions. I also thank the libraries of the University of North Carolina at Chapel Hill, especially for giving me access to various electronic data bases. In particular, I am grateful to the librarian of the Cathedral Library of Valencia, Spain, for providing me with a xerox copy of MS 184 and to Prof. Ciriaco M. Arroyo for applying on my behalf; and to Dr Margaret Jennings for providing me with a xerox copy of John of Wales's *Ars faciendi sermones* in Ulm 1480. Lastly, I warmly thank Jackie Brown for supervising with great care and promptness the publication program of the Medieval Academy of America at a moment of crisis.

Abbreviations

Throughout this book the medieval works whose teaching is here synthesized are referred to by the names of their authors, titles, or incipits in abbreviated form (Thetford, Ars copiosa, Vade). They are in alphabetical order.

Ad erudicionem	Anonymous, "Ad erudicionem"
Ad habendum	Anonymous, "Ad habendum materiam in predicacionibus"
Alan	Alanus of Lille, *Summa de arte praedicatoria*
Alcok	Simon Alcok, *Tractatus de modo dividendi thema pro materia dilatanda*
Alprão	Alfonso d'Alprão, *Ars praedicandi, conferendi, collationandi, arengandi*
Antoninus	Antoninus of Florence, *Summa theologica*
Ars copiosa	Anonymous, *Ars copiosa*
Ashby	Alexander of Ashby, *De artificioso modo predicandi*
Auvergne	William of Auvergne, *Ars praedicandi*
Basevorn	Robert of Basevorn, *Forma praedicandi*
Borgsleben	Christian Borgsleben, *Ars predicandi*
Chobham	Thomas of Chobham, *Summa de arte praedicandi*
Circa	Anonymous, *Ars faciendi sermonem*, "Circa artem"
Cordoba	Martin of Cordoba, *Ars praedicandi*
Dic	Anonymous, "Dic nobis"
Eiximenes	Francesc Eiximenes, *Modus sermocinandi*

Exercitacio	Anonymous, *Exercitacio in collacionibus*, "Si quis wlt exercitari"
Fusignano	Jacobus de Fusignano, *Libellus artis predicatorie*
Hesse	Henry of Hesse, *Tractatulus de arte praedicandi valde utilis*
Hic docet	Anonymous, "Hic docet Augustinus"
Higden	Ranulph Higden, *Ars componendi sermones*
In accepcione	Anonymous, *De modo sermonizandi*, "In accepcione thematis"
In predicatore	Anonymous, "In predicatore"
Lull	Ramon Lull, *Liber de praedicatione*
Nota	Anonymous, "Nota pro arte faciendi"
Omnis	Anonymous, *Ars sermocinandi utilis, breuis et ualde bona pro introducendis rudibus in ea*, "Omnis rei inicio"
Piscario	Geraldus de Piscario, *Ars faciendi sermones*
Predicacio	Anonymous, *Forma predicandi*, "Predicacio est thematis assumpcio"
Ps.-Aquinas	Ps.-Aquinas, *Tractatulus solemnis de arte et vero modo predicandi*
Ps.-Bonaventure	Ps.-Bonaventure, *Ars concionandi*
Quamvis	Anonymous, *De sermonibus pertractandis*, "Quamvis de sermonibus faciendis"
Rochelle	Jean de la Rochelle, *Processus negociandi themata sermonum*
Schale	Geoffrey Schale, "Fecunda gracia Saluatoris"
Si vis	Anonymous, "Si vis sermonem ex arte conficere"
Thetford	Richard of Thetford, *Ars dilatandi sermones*
Tuderto	Thomas de Tuderto, *Ars sermocinandi ac collationes faciendi*
Vade	Anonymous, "Vade in domum tuam"
Wales	John of Wales, *Ars faciendi sermones*
Waleys	Thomas Waleys, *De theoria sive arte praedicandi*

The works appear in roughly chronological order in the Table of Contents as well as in sections 2–43, and they are listed in that order in the documentation of the respective topics in section 45. In addition, the following abbreviations occur in the text with some regularity:

BL	British Library
Caplan	Harry Caplan, *Mediaeval "Artes Praedicandi": A Hand-List.* Cornell Studies in Classical Philology 24 (Ithaca: Cornell University Press, 1934).
Caplan Suppl	Harry Caplan, *Mediaeval "Artes Praedicandi": A Supplementary Hand-List.* Cornell Studies in Classical Philology 25 (Ithaca: Cornell University Press, 1936)
CCSL	Corpus Christianorum, Series Latina (Turnhout: Brepols)
Charland	Th.-M. Charland, *Artes Praedicandi: Contribution à l'histoire de la rhétorique au moyen âge* (Paris: De Vrin, 1936)
CUL	Cambridge, University Library
ODNB	Oxford Dictionary of National Biography, electronic version (Oxford and New York: Oxford University Press, 2004–)
OESA	Ordo Eremitarum Sancti Augustini
OFM	Ordo Fratrum Minorum
OFMCap	Ordo Fratrum Minorum Cappucinorum
OSA	Ordo Sancti Augustini
OSB	Ordo Sancti Benedicti
OP	Ordo Fratrum Praedicatorum
PL	J.P. Migne, ed., *Patrologiae cursus completus. Series latina*, 217 vols. (Paris: J.P. Migne, 1844–64)
Sharpe	Richard Sharpe, *A Handlist of the Latin Writers of Great Britain and Ireland Before 1540* (Turnhout: Brepols, 1997), quoted by page number

For the abbreviated references to other works cited in the notes (author and date of publication), see the section "Works Cited" below, pp. 117–25.

Introduction

Theologians and preachers of Western Europe from the early thirteenth to the late fifteenth century developed and used a peculiar sermon form variously referred to as the modern, university, thematic, or scholastic sermon.[1] Typically, it begins with a short biblical text, divides it into several parts, and then develops the latter at greater or shorter length. These basic elements of thema, division, and development form a religious discourse that differs structurally from what is commonly called the homily, in which a biblical text, usually a longer lection, is explained, often along the four senses that Scripture can have, and applied to the moral life of Christians. The homily form, prevalent among the Church Fathers and preachers before roughly 1200, continued in use to the end of the Middle Ages and beyond. But in the manuscripts that have preserved the rhetorical efforts of later medieval preachers the overwhelming majority of sermons are built on the scholastic model. This form was also taught in treatises of varying length, the *artes praedicandi*, whose major aim was to instruct beginning preachers in composing their sermons in conformity with the "modern" usage.[2]

Harry Caplan, with the help of several co-workers, established a list of medieval treatises of this kind that comprises over 230 numbered items (Caplan and Caplan Suppl). Of these, about thirty are available in modern editions. They form a corpus sufficient for modern readers

1 See further below, pp. 47–50.

2 The scholastic sermon form has been described many times. Substantial descriptions can be found in: Gilson 1932; Charland pp. 109–226 (following Basevorn); Ross 1940, pp. xliii–li; and more briefly Wenzel 2005, pp. 86–7.

and scholars to gain an adequate notion of what the typical scholastic sermon form as taught in these manuals was like. Yet at the same time it is clear to anyone who peruses several of them that these works possess individual features that distinguish one from another, certainly in their form of presentation and often in specific details. With only a relatively small numbers of manuals available in print, we are certainly not yet able to see the whole picture. Hence, there is a very real demand simply to make more treatises of this kind accessible in critical editions. Such editions should be informed by a precise knowledge, on the part of their editors, of scholastic sermon structure, its concerns, and its vocabulary. It will, obviously, not do to uncritically reproduce scribal errors and misreadings.

There is a further aspect to the study of medieval sacred rhetoric and the teaching which these *artes praedicandi* provide: the desire and in fact the need to discern their interrelationships, the dependence and influence of individual works, and the entire development that led from such early *artes* as Chobham to late-medieval representatives of the genre, such as the anonymous Circa. Franco Morenzoni, who has critically studied and edited a number of key works of the kind, has said that studying this literature is in many respects a very risky undertaking, *une entreprise fort risquée*, because the manuscripts in which they have been preserved and their individual histories have not been carefully investigated. At this point, any attempt at a synthesis of the medieval art of preaching must be premature.[3] There is, then, a real need, not only for more texts but additionally for precise investigations of their manuscripts, their contexts, their interdependencies. To mention only one question that must be addressed: what does it mean that in many cases a single manuscript contains not one but two or three or even more of these *artes*, and these are often substantively very different from each other?[4]

Yet a synthesis of a different kind from what Morenzoni had in mind is in fact possible: a systematic and orderly survey of what the *artes* teach about sermon structure. This the present book intends to provide. For it

---

3 Morenzoni 1995, p. 339. Margaret Jennings has, in several articles, attempted to trace a history and development of the *artes praedicandi*, with attention to their putative relation to Cicero's rhetorical works (see especially Jennings 1989 and Jennings 2006). But compare Morenzoni 1988, pp. xlviii–lxiv.

4 See Wenzel 2013a, pp. 110–11.

is clear that on the one hand their authors shared a common notion of what a good scholastic sermon should look like, while on the other it is equally clear that they differ – sometimes substantially – in discussing specific details. The following sections will therefore, first, briefly introduce the works considered (sections 1–43), then examine their teaching following the order of a scholastic sermon (sections 44–7), and finally discuss some marginal issues implied (sections 48–50).

This book is, therefore, not a history of the scholastic sermon, let alone of medieval preaching, but a structural analysis of the scholastic sermon as taught by the *artes*; it aims at fostering interest in medieval *artes praedicandi* and at serving as a guide to readers and researchers of texts that are very often dense, confusing, and hard to penetrate.[5] Any reader who has tackled some of the longer works available in modern editions, especially those by Thomas Waleys and Robert of Basevorn, can testify how easy it is to lose one's way and one's interest, partly because of their difficult technical vocabulary and partly because of their not always straightforward progression. [6]

In addition, this synthesis will also show that despite the common *Gestalt* they follow and describe, these works differ from each other. Such differences lie, first, in their approach and style. Some *artes* describe, others command, and yet others mix these modes of presentation. Some build a system with the help of numbering and logical relationships, others use a dominant image, such as a tree or a house, to structure their teaching. Second, the works also differ in specific matters they teach. For example, later *artes* show a greater, more refined interest than earlier ones in the way the sermon division is introduced – what I shall call the "bridge passage" – and even employ a special word for it, *pes* or *positio pedis*, whose usage is not recorded in Latin dictionaries. I find it quite remarkable how much individual authors of these works, whether they are known by name or remain anonymous, go their own way. This is particularly true of their choosing a specific biblical thema for their illustrations; one gains the impression that authors of *artes praedicandi* may have known the works of their predecessors and tried

5 For an illustration of how knowledge of the scholastic sermon form can help to understand a manuscript that has baffled scholars for years, see Wenzel 1995.

6 It might be considered unfortunate that Charland chose Basevorn's treatise for his exposition of scholastic sermon structure and that, probably for that reason, this particularly difficult work is one of the very few *artes* available in an English translation (Krul, in Murphy 1971, pp. 109–215).

to avoid using the same illustrations. As a consequence, where one finds the same thema used in different works, one will have to think of dependency of one *ars* on another, or else suspect some common teaching, probably at the university. But to unravel all this is exactly the kind of scholarly investigation asked for by Morenzoni and others, for which these sections are intended to furnish some help.

PART I

The *Artes*

1 *Artes praedicandi*

If used to describe a particular literary genre,[7] the label *ars praedicandi* refers to a work that deals with preaching, not letter-writing or poetry or logical argumentation, and presents itself as a treatise that describes and gives guidance – in other words furnishes a technique (*ars*) – for that activity. To do this it may embrace a multitude of aspects including the preacher's moral life and study, his articulation and gestures while preaching, and the actual form of his sermon. The extant medieval works that are thus labelled by modern scholars deal with such aspects, even if not all of them contain them all. One can, therefore, distinguish between several types;

(a) comprehensive *artes praedicandi*, which do all these things,
(b) complete ones, which deal only with sermon structure,
(c) limited ones, which treat only a single aspect of this sermon structure, such as ways of development.

The following sections (2–43) introduce some forty *artes praedicandi* of whatever type, whose teaching on sermon structure is here synthesized. Most of them are available in modern editions, to which I have added a number that remain unedited and have come to my attention in reading manuscripts containing medieval Latin sermons. They appear here in roughly chronological order, as far as that can be determined, with the exception of the treatise by Ramon Lull, which stands at the end because of the idiosyncracies of Ramon's general system, of which his *ars praedicandi* forms part. I cite these works in a shortened form (listed above, pp. xi–xii), except for the works by Guibert of Nogent, Guibert of Tournai, and Humbert of Romans, which are not of the same importance for this synthesis.

All the works here introduced will be briefly identified by their authors, with particular attention to their religious affiliation (unless the works are anonymous) and their listing in Caplan, Caplan Suppl, and Charland, including a reference to the number of known manuscripts that have preserved them. Since frequently two or more *artes*

7 "Art of preaching" may of course also refer to the act of preaching itself or the performance of techniques taught by such treatises.

appear together in the same manuscript, I have added that information where it applies. This will be followed by a summary or characterization of their contents. And finally each section will list modern editions of these works, their translations, significant discussions by previous scholars, and the source to which the following sections refer.

2 Guibert of Nogent

OSB, died 1124.

Liber quo ordine sermo fieri debeat, "Valde illi periculosum est a doctrina cessare."

Not in Caplan or Charland.

Despite its title the treatise does not deal with the structure of the public sermon but is an exhortation to preach, both orally and evidently in writing, for the moral benefit of others, emphasizing the need to discuss vices (for greater self-knowledge) and to understand Scripture in its four senses.

Edition: PL 156:21–32.

Translation: Miller 1969.

Discussion: Murphy 1974, pp. 299–303.

Citations from PL by column.

3 Alan of Lille (Alan)

Secular theologian, entered the Cistercian order near the end of his life; died 1203.

Summa de arte praedicatoria, "Vidit scalam Jacob ... Praedicatio est manifesta."

Not in Caplan or Charland. But notice that Caplan 199 and Suppl 199 list a work or works that begin with the same definition of *praedicatio;* as does Charland 103.

Many manuscripts; see D'Alverny 1965, pp. 109–91.

Occurs with Thetford in Oxford, Bodleian Library, MS Bodley 848.

In the preface Alan (or Alanus) moralizes his initial quotation of Jacob's ladder (Genesis 28:12) as the seven rungs or steps on the way of perfection, from confession to preaching. His treatise is devoted to the last step, and Alan announces that he will deal with (I) what preaching a sermon means,[8] (II) who is to preach, (III) to whom he is to preach, (IV) why, and (V) where he is to preach. Only the first three parts are developed (in the edition), in a total of 48 chapters. Though the entire work is of wider scope than the preaching arts here synthesized, it contains a brief section on *forma praedicationis*, which includes such aspects of scholastic sermon technique as the use of a proper thema, here called *auctoritas*, which forms the *fundamentum* of a sermon; a *captatio benevolentiae*; exposition of the authority, with the use of other authorities including the sayings of *gentiles*; and proving one's points with *exempla* (chapter 1, PL 210:113–14). To illustrate this, Alan discusses a number of moral topics (contempt of the world, vices, virtues, confession, etc.), for each of which he provides one or more fitting "authorities" (chapters 2–37). Occasionally the latter are quotations from the Fathers (e.g., Jerome, in chapter 28). These illustrative chapters contain such techniques as division, distinction, confirmation, proof, and development including emotive language, address of the audience, quotations from (pagan) poets, etc. After briefly discussing the qualities required of a preacher (part II, chapter 38), Alan addresses the question to whom one is to preach (part III, chapter 39) and then provides further authorities and material that may be useful in preaching to various social groups and *status* (knights, lawyers, priests, virgins, etc.; chapters 39–48).

Edition: PL 210:111–98.

Translation: Evans 1981.

Discussion: Murphy 1974, pp. 303–9; Briscoe 1992, pp. 20–5.

Citations from PL 210 by column.

4 Alexander of Ashby (Ashby)

Augustinian canon (OSA), at Canons Ashby (or Esseby), Northamptonshire; died 1208 or 1214.

De artificioso modo predicandi, "Venerabili abbati salutem et dilectionem in Christo. Iocundum humane infirmitatis solatium ... In omni scriptura et sermone."

8 His definition is: "The open and public instruction in morals and faith, serving to inform the people, deriving from the way of reason and the fountain of authorities" (Manifesta et publica instructio morum et fidei, informationi hominum deserviens, ex rationum semita et auctoritatum fonte proveniens, 111).

Caplan 67, corrected in Caplan Suppl 67. Charland 23. To the four copies listed in Sharpe 47, Morenzoni 2004 adds two more at the Benediktinerstift of Melk (pp. 18–19).

Occurs with Thetford in Oxford, Magdalen College, MS 168.

The prologue is directed to an unnamed abbot who, after being a promising scholar, had abandoned his studies and the practice of preaching when he entered the order, but now as abbot (or perhaps rather "prior"?) has the duty to preach to his community. Alexander sends him this treatise so that he may "be kindled to love teaching and delight in his office of teaching the more he learns how to teach in an artful manner (*artificiosius*)." After dealing with the *prohemium* – which must render the audience docile, benevolent, and attentive – the author briefly discusses the fact that the preacher must consider what he is saying to whom (i.e., the nature of his audience), how he is to speak (his subject matter and his way of presentation), and how much he is to say. The second point, the way of speaking (*modus dicendi*), is then treated at greater length. It considers four parts of the sermon: prologue, division, confirmation, and conclusion. Before the prologue the preacher is to give an authority (*auctoritas*) that should contain the matter of the entire sermon. After dealing with the conclusion, Alexander adds a brief section on delivery (*pronuntiatio*) and a final reflection on rhetorical embellishment (*venustas verborum*). The work quotes Gregory the Great several times at some length, as well as Horace. The treatise itself is devoid of illustrations; instead it is followed by five sample sermons.

Edition: Morenzoni 1991 and Morenzoni 2004, pp. 21–33.

Discussion: Murphy 1974, pp. 312–17 (summary and debt to Cicero); Morenzoni 1991, pp. 891–4; Donavin 1997.

Citations from Morenzoni 2004 by page.

5 Thomas of Chobham (Chobham)

Secular clergy, subdean of Salisbury Cathedral, died after 1233 (see Goering 2004). *Summa de arte praedicandi*, "Humane nature conditio … Post hec ad euidenciam ordinis dicendorum" (before 1221).

Not in Caplan. Charland 91 (Thomas de Salisbury, no mss). Morenzoni 1988 lists 2 manuscripts (pp. lxv–lxvi).

This long, occasionally long-winded treatise (300 pages in print) consists of a prologue and seven parts. The prologue discusses the *modus significandi in theologia* and cites the seven rules of Tyconius. In the next sections Thomas gives (i) a definition of preaching[9] and then deals with (ii) kinds of preaching (five), (iii) who may and must preach, (iv) what is to be preached, (v) to whom one is to preach, (vi) the subject matter of preaching (vices and virtues), and (vii) the art of preaching. Only the last (i.e., seventh) section, entitled *De arte predicandi*, is directly relevant to this study. It has two parts. Following a short comparison between "comics" (i.e., dramatists), poets, and preachers, and declaring that like orators, preachers speak to persuade people to the good and dissuade them from what is evil, Thomas concludes that oratorical knowledge is necessary for the office of a preacher (valde necessaria est doctrina oratoris ad officium predicatoris, 262; see also 294). With that he discusses (I) the parts of a speech or *oratio*: *exordium, narratio, divisio, confirmatio, confutatio, conclusio*; (II) the parts of rhetoric: *inventio, dispositio, elocutio, memoria,* and *pronuntiatio.* Thomas thus reconciles scholastic sermon structure with the precepts of classical rhetoric as set forth by Cicero and the *Ad Herennium,* both of which are quoted constantly (usually with *philosophus* as their author), as is Seneca. Part II is the longest section that deals with sermon structure. Especially in its section on *inventio* (269–96) Thomas discusses at some leisure and illustrates much of what in later *artes* becomes commonplace. In both (I) and (II) he uses technical terms that are characteristic of scholastic sermon structure, such as *prothema,* thema, *distinctio, prosecutio,* and the final *oratio.*

Edition: Morenzoni 1988.

Translation in part in Copeland and Sluiter 2009, pp. 616–38.

Discussion: Murphy 1974, pp. 317–26; Morenzoni 1988, esp. pp. lviii–lxiv.

Citations from Morenzoni 1988 by page.

6 Richard of Thetford (Thetford)

Affiliation uncertain (monastic?). Thirteenth century.

Ars dilatandi sermones, "Quoniam aemulatores estis spirituum ad aedificationem ecclesiae, quaerite ut habundetis. Bene dicit *aemulatores* et non simulators ... Sunt autem plures modi." (Variant: "Octo sunt modi ...").

9 "Preaching is announcing the word of God for the instruction in faith and morals" (Est igitur praedicatio diuini verbi ad informationem fidei et morum nuntiatio, 15).

Caplan 154 (21 mss; see also other initia, ibidem). Charland 77–80 (26 mss). Extant also in abbreviations or summaries; see Sharpe 514–15.

Occurs with Waleys in Basel, Universitätsbibliothek, MS B.x.9; Omnis in Oxford, Balliol College, MS 179; Alan in Oxford, Bodleian Library, MS Bodley 848; and Ashby in Oxford, Magdalen College, MS 168.

Judging by the number of surviving copies, this treatise was one of the most popular arts of preaching; some of its material also appears in other *artes*, such as Basevorn. After applying the five key terms of the initial quotation (1 Corinthians 14:12) to the work of preaching, Thetford focuses more narrowly on "many [*variant*: eight] modes by which a preacher may abound and dilate his sermon." These are described and illustrated with examples: (I) explaining a noun or name with a sentence, by definition, description, or etymology (*interpretatio*); (II) division of a concept (what other *artes* more properly call *distinctio*) with confirmation; (III) giving an argument; (IV) with fitting (*concordantes*) proof texts; (V) with different grammatical forms of the same word (degrees of comparison; compound verbs); (VI) developing the properties of an object; (VII) using the four senses of Scripture; (VIII) indicating causes and effects. In all of this, the preacher should always concentrate on the virtues and vices. Then Thetford shows where in Scripture these modes can be found and what may help the preacher in employing them. In giving examples of "etymology," he considers not only words of Greek and Latin origin but also English and French ones, and he gives further explanations amd illustrations of the eight preceding sections and adds some other devices.

In some manuscripts Thetford is the third part of a longer treatise on preaching, Ps.-Bonaventure (see the following section).

Edition: As part III of the *Ars concionandi* sometimes attributed to Bonaventure, in Bonaventure 1901, pp. 16–21. Superseded. Edition and translation: Engelhard 1978 (with variants).

Discussion: Murphy 1974, pp. 326–9; Roth 1956, pp. 71–5.

Citations from Engelhard 1978 by page.

7 Ps.-Bonaventure, *Ars concionandi* (Ps.-Bonaventure)

Anonymous, ascribed to Bonaventure in one ms.

Ars concionandi, "Omnis tractatio scripturarum, ut ait Augustinus" (and variants).

Caplan 114. Charland 30–3. In one form or another, the work is extant in at least 11 mss.

In some manuscripts, Thetford is combined with two other works, thus forming the third part of a unified treatise on preaching, whose first part is Ps.-Bonaventure. The *Prooemium* to the whole treatise declares that according to St Augustine, the preacher's work consists in finding what is to be learned and in presenting what he has learned. He must be intent on (1) divisions (which establish *proprietas*, for instruction), (2) distinctions (*brevitas*, for delighting), and (3) development (*utilitas*, for "bending" the audience's emotions). In other words, the anonymous author relates three major aspects of sermon making to Augustine's triple purpose of rhetoric: *docere, delectare, flectere.*[10] The first part of this work (i.e., Ps.-Bonaventure) then deals with making the division; the second, which is very short, with the distinction; and the third (i.e., Thetford), with the development or dilatation.

Ps.-Bonaventure contains twenty-eight sections that discuss various aspects of the division. It demands that before making the division one must examine the meaning of the chosen thema and, especially, to whom its words are directed and their specific mode (question, call, exhortation, etc.). It further includes the distinction between *divisio intra* and *extra*. These sections teach, not so much by definition and discussion as by giving a wealth of illustrative examples.

Edition: Bonaventure 1901, pp. 8–16.

Translation: Hazel 1972a.

Discussion: Hazel 1972b and Hazel 1973; Murphy 1974, pp. 329–30; Briscoe 1992, pp. 32–5; Roth, pp. 65–76 (the best).

Citations from Bonaventure 1901 by page.

8 William of Auvergne (Auvergne)

Secular theologian, bishop of Paris, died 1249.

Ars praedicandi, "Verbum Dei propter Christum et non questum, propter Deum, non denarium praedicare volentibus" (spurious).

Caplan 179 and Caplan Suppl 179 (total of 15 mss; to which add: Augsburg, Universitätsbibliothek, Cod. II.1); Charland 39–42.

10 Augustine, *De doctrina Christiana* 4.12.27, in Augustine, *De doctrina Christiana*, ed. and trans. R.P.H. Green (Oxford, 1995), p. 228; cf. Cicero, *Brutus* 185, in Cicero, *Brutus*, ed. E. Malcovati (Leipzig, 1970), p. 55. See also its use in the sample sermon below (p. 89).

William of Auvergne wrote several theological works that touch upon preaching, especially *De faciebus mundi*, which discusses material for use in sermons and may lie behind the technical term *facies* used by several *artes praedicandi*.[11] The *Ars praedicandi* here listed has been shown not to be by him (Morenzoni 2005, pp. 293–5, and Morenzoni 2006, p. 252). It begins with short answers to the questions of who, what, to whom, where, when, and how one is to preach, and then announces and develops twenty equally short chapters that range from a brief praise of preaching, through the demand to adapt one's style to one's audience and to preach with emotion, to several specific techniques of development, such as division, distinction, name etymology, use of acrostics, etc., but without giving a systematic account of the scholastic sermon structure.

Edition: De Poorter 1923.

Discussion: Murphy 1974, pp. 330–2; Roth 1956, pp. 48–54.

Citations from De Poorter 1923 by page.

9 Jean de la Rochelle (Rochelle)

OFM, Paris master, died 1245.

Processus negociandi themata sermonum, "Cum plures sint modi negociandi circa themata."

Caplan 31 and Caplan Suppl 31 (one manuscript complete with ascription, two others incomplete). Charland 62–4.

Occurs with In predicatore and Exercitacio in London, BL, MS Arundel 275; and with Wales, Eiximenes, Lull, and others in Vatican, MS Ottoboni 396.

The work announces and treats seven ways of dealing with the thema "in order to avoid errors": (I) developing "root" and "branches" from the thema; (II) dealing with a thema that contains a second-person word form; (III) developing it by quoting an authority that states the opposite and dividing the latter; (IV) when in the thema a notion is expressed by different words or things, as by a simile or parable; (V) when, on the contrary, a word in the thema can have different meanings; (VI) developing the thema by quoting and dividing an authority with the same

11 See below, section 45-j.

meaning, as against (III); (VII) developing an authority in more than one way, in which case the individual expositions must have the same number of members. Hence, this treatise deals basically with the division and development of a scriptural authority, paying close attention to specific (grammatical) situations and illustrating each case.

A rarity in this work is a long list of notional pairs or triads that belong to a series of such categories as status, condition, etc., to which "all the parts placed in the sermon according to this mode [i.e., (II) above] must be reduced." The same list appears in Ars copiosa and may indicate the latter's dependence on Rochelle.

Edition: Cantini 1951.

New edition and translation: Wenzel 2013b, pp. 189–239.

Discussion: Murphy 1974, p. 330 (superseded).

Citations from Wenzel 2013b by page (the Latin text, English translation on the next page).

10 Guibert of Tournai

OFM, Paris master 1259–61.

Not in Caplan or Charland. 3 mss (and 2 lost) noted in Gieben 1988.

Guibert produced a vast treatise on spiritual teaching, called *Rudimentum* (or *Erudimentum*) *doctrinae* (between 1259 and 1268), written in different stages and as yet unedited. It is accompanied by a detailed outline called *Registrum*. The latter indicates that the work consisted of four main parts following the four Aristotelian causes. Part II (*causa efficiens*), on the various sources that provide doctrine (from God to preachers), contained in its sixth subpart a discussion of preachers and their qualifications and, in title 6, dealt with dilatation of the sermon matter (i.e., the thema?). This provides four modes: definition according to the four causes; division; reasoning; and exposition in various ways including subdivision. This is followed by 100 themata for sermons, of which eighty-seven are *ad status* and thirteen on theological subjects (such as the sacraments, baptism, commandments, etc.). Apparently these are themata for actual sermons that were to appear in the *Rudimentum*, but so far have not been found.

Unedited; but see Gieben 1988, pp. 646–89, for the *Registrum*.

Discussion Gieben 1988; D'Avray 1985, pp. 144–6

Citations from Gieben 1988 by page.

11 Humbert of Romans

OP, General of the order (1254–63), died 1277.

De eruditione religiosorum praedicatorum, "Vide ministerium quod accepisti ... Solet contingere."

Not in Caplan. Charland 47.

A treatise on preaching in general, containing two books. The first (A) deals with the office of preaching, qualifications of the preacher, etc., and includes scattered remarks about sermon technique, especially on the protheme. The second (B) provides 200 model sermons *ad status* and for various occasions.

Edition: Humbert 1739; Humbert 1889.

Translation: Humbert 1951; Tugwell 1982, pp. 183–370 (selections).

Discussion: Roth 1956, pp. 57–64; Tugwell 1989; Tugwell 1993.

12 John of Wales (Wales)

OFM, died 1285. Produced several popular works for the use of preachers. See Swanson 1989 and Swanson 2004.

Ars faciendi sermones, "In isto libello quatuor capitula continentur." A variant beginning: "Ad peticionem cuiusdam predilecti me satisfaciendum."

Caplan 62 and Caplan Suppl 62 (*In isto*: 12 mss and incunables); Caplan 7 and Caplan Suppl 7 (*Ad peticionem*: 7 mss). Charland 55–60 (the *Moniloquium* he discusses is not an *ars praedicandi*). Cf. Sharpe 340.

Occurs with Rochelle, Eiximenes, Lull, and others in Vatican Library, MS Ottoboni 396.

The four chapters announced at the beginning (a section which is not in the incunable edition) discuss: (I) four different kinds of sermon; (II) the definition of "preaching" or "sermon" (*predicacio*); (III) various rules for making a proper sermon; and (IV) differences between different kinds of sermons (occasion, audience). The distinction of four kinds in chapter I is based on the relation between the thema and its immediate development, in terms of (a) notional and (b) verbal agreement, thus yielding the following kinds: a and b; a alone; b alone; neither a nor b. These are useful to different kinds of preachers, audiences, or occasions. John will base his further exposition of the first kind, that of *moderni auctores*. The long chapter II then gives a definition of *predicacio*:

"Preaching [*or* the sermon] is, after invoking divine help, the clear and devout exposition of the announced thema by dividing, subdividing, and establishing concordances for it, for the Catholic instruction of the intellect and the charitable formation of the affect."[12] The terms of this definition are then explained by way of the four Aristotelian causes, after which John treats the parts of a scholastic sermon from protheme to subdivision, with much illustration. Chaper III adds several additional considerations or rules about dealing with proof texts and their agreement. Chapter IV speaks briefly of three kinds of sermons, those for Sundays, for feast days, and *ad status*, to which John adds even more briefly a list of books necessary for preaching, and several different ways that are used "now" in university preaching.

The versions of this work preserved in manuscripts and incunables show many differences in detail, often significant ones, and a critical study with edition of this important and popular work is much needed.

Edition: Only incunables; I have used that of Ulm (?) 1480.

Discussion: Roth 1956, pp. 76–86 (good summary with quotations); Zafarana 1981, pp. 223–4, 230–1, 243 (some quotations); Murphy 1974, pp. 332–3; Briscoe 1992, pp. 36–7.

Citations from Ulm 1480 by folio; but notice that the text in the incunable edition is shorter than that of Vatican Library, MS Ottoboni 396.

13 Predicacio est (Predicacio)

Anonymous.

Forma predicandi, "Predicacio est thematis assumpcio."

Caplan 121 and Caplan Suppl 121 (6 manuscripts, all English). Charland 57–8. In an additional manuscript the work is amalgamated with Quamvis (q.v.): Cambridge, Corpus Christi College, MS 423.

Occurs with Ad habendum in London, BL, MS Harley 1615; and with Fusignano and Quamvis in Oxford, University College, MS 36.

12 "Predicatio est inuocato diuino auxilio diuidendo, subdiuidendo, et concordando propositi thematis clara et deuota expositio ad intellectus catholicam instructionem et affectus caritatiuam informationem" (18). The definition and subsequent listing of the sermon parts are also reproduced in Ross 1937, p. 340, n. 18.

This very short treatise (93 lines in the printed edition), evidently based on Wales, defines "preaching" or "sermon" (*predicacio*) in terms of its constituent parts: "Preaching [*or* the sermon] is the taking up of a thema, the division of this thema, the subdivision of the divided thema, the fitting quotation of concording authorities, and the clear and devout explanation of these quoted authorities, to worship the Lord widely, illuminate the Church Militant, and bend the human affect towards God."[13] It then briefly lists the sermon parts again in the order of their appearance in the sermon: thema, *antethema*, prayer for divine help, repetition of the thema, introduction to the thema, division, subdivision, confirmation of the parts, and explanation of the parts. This is followed by an example.

Edition: Ross 1937.

Discussion: Murphy 1974, p. 333.

Citations from Ross 1937 by page.

14 Ad habendum materiam (Ad habendum)

Anonymous, apparently by a Franciscan, thirteenth century.

"Ad habendum materiam in praedicationibus in thematibus sciendum quod praedicatur decem modis."[14]

Caplan 1 and Caplan Suppl 1 (total of 9 mss). Charland 96 (10 mss). Add Cambridge, Gonville and Caius College, MS 439 (Gieben 1962).

Occurs with Predicacio in London, BL, MS Harley 1615; with Quamvis in Utrecht, University Library, MS 317.

This short work lists and illustrates ten ways of developing the thema: (I) definition and description; (II) division; (III) argument; (IV) fitting proof texts from Scripture, saints, and moral philosopers; (V) comparative degrees; (VI) properties of objects; (VII) cause or effect; (VIII) fourfold sense of Scripture; (IX) progressing through several words in the thema; (X) combining words of the thema in several ways. These modes

13 "Predicacio est thematis assumpcio, eiusdem thematis diuisio, thematis diuisi subdiuisio, concordanciarum congrua cotacio, et auctoritatum adductarum clara et deuota explanacio, ad Domini cultus amplitudinem, ecclesie militantis illustracionem, et humani affectus erga Deum inclinacionem" (340–1).

14 *Pace* the listings in Caplan and Charland, the incipit in Utrecht 317 clearly reads *habendum*, which would be standard medieval practice.

and their respective illustrations are the same as those given by Cordoba in its chapter on dilation (see below).

Edition and discussion: Gieben 1962.

Citations from Gieben 1962 by page.

15 Robert of Basevorn (Basevorn)

Secular (?), c. 1322.

Forma praedicandi, "Dominus mihi astitit ... Sicut dicit Philosophus, periti ... Ostendendum est imprimis quid est praedicatio ..."

Caplan 116 (5 mss, one bearing Basevorn's name and dating the tabula for the work in 1322). Charland 81–2.

In the prologue to this long and rich treatise, Basevorn gives the usual reasons for writing, such as pressure from clerics to write about preaching, leisure, and the desire to avoid idleness. He tells us that when he came upon the initial biblical quote ("The Lord stood by me and strengthened me, that by me the preaching may be accomplished," 2 Timothy 4:17) he gained confidence; and then he applies the quotation to the four (Aristotelian) causes of preaching. A table follows, in which he lists fifty chapters that range from a definition of *praedicatio* and the qualities required in a preacher to twenty-two *ornamenta sermonis*, which include the main features of the scholastic sermon. *Praedicatio* is defined as persuasive speech directed to many people in order to gain spiritual merit and being of moderate length,[15] which distinguishes it from theological determination as well as from (private) admonition, and further from various kinds of public speech (I). Basevorn next deals with such topics as who may canonically preach and who may be properly called a preacher, including comments on *quaestuarii* (such as Chaucer's Pardoner) and "limitours" (II–V). He looks at different sermon forms used by God in the Old Testament, Christ, and the saints (VI–XIII), declaring that "there are almost as many different forms of preaching as there are preachers" (VI). In reviewing major preachers of the past, Basevorn praises St Bernard for preaching "artfully" (*artificialiter*) and using thema, introduction, division, confirmation, and conclusion (XII). Bernard and other saints also combined wisdom in their preaching with

15 "Est autem praedicatio pluribus facta persuasio ad merendum, moderatum tempus retinens" (238).

eloquence (XIII). Then Basevorn continues (XIV) to list twenty-two sermon "ornaments" that are used by modern preachers, which he treats seriatim (XV–L). They include the main structural features of a scholastic sermon (XV–XLVII). To them Basevorn adds some further remarks about dividing the thema and analyses two additional modes that can be useful for lay or clerical audiences respectively (XLIX–L). In chapter L he declares that, as he has shown, modern preachers utilize twenty-four different modes of sermon structure, and he briefly discusses seven "more external ornaments," such as the use of rhyme and other rhetorical colours, modulation of the voice, gestures, joking, and so on (L). Chapters XXVII–XXX recommend themata for sermons *de tempore, de sanctis,* for special occasions, and *ad status,* which in Charland's edition are reproduced only selectively.

Among the *artes praedicandi* on which this synthesis is based, Basevorn's treatise clearly stands out by its individuality and sophistication. Not only is he merely aware of different modes of preaching but he can sharply distinguish between styles used at Paris and at Oxford and give pertinent illustrations. He also offers many personal remarks of approval or disapproval. At the same time, his speaking of "ornaments" is unique and does not quite reflect what one may consider the standard treatment of scholastic sermon structure found elsewhere. Moreover, by its very sophistication his treatment can be confusing and hard to follow. At one point, for example, he uses the term "thema" equivocally for the entire main part of the sermon, distinguishing it from the *antethema,* which likewise includes several steps (268). Or the discussion of *confirmatio* leads him to analyse Paris preaching in such a way that he soon finds himself talking about the sermon development (284–90).

Edition: Charland, pp. 233–323.
Translation: L. Krul, in Murphy 1971, pp. 109–215.
Discussion: Murphy 1974, pp. 343–55 (with a detailed outline); Briscoe 1992, pp. 37–40; Wenzel 2005a, p. 220 (on the sermons in London, BL, MS Additional 38818).
Citations from Charland by page.

16 Geraldus de Piscario (Piscario)

OFM, Toulouse, 1330s.
Ars faciendi sermones, "Quesivisti [*var.* Petisti] a me."
Caplan 140 and Caplan Suppl 140 (7 mss). Charland 27–8 (under "Astazius").

In answering the question "whether one can find some special technique in building collations and sermons," the author announces and then develops eight parts: (I) choosing a thema and making a statement about what it connotes; this is followed by several features that distinguish a sermon from a collation; (II) relations between the words of the thema and of the division; (III) aspects of subdivision and distinction, especially the distinction according to the four senses of Scripture; (IV) the agreement between a part of the division and the proof text that is to confirm it; (V) development of the sermon, considering especially introductions (*introytus*) to different sections and subdivision of proof texts, and giving other advice about preaching in general; (VI) different ways of preaching: the *sancti doctores* of the past vs. *moderni*; preaching about the entire gospel lection without a specific thema, *postillatio*, etc.; developing an extended allegory of castles with towers, knights with shields and weapons, etc. (which Geraldus condemns as unscriptural); (VII) how to find appropriate words and combine them; this is the longest part of the treatise, in twelve sections, and includes lists of words with the same ending; (VIII) how to multiply words with the help of a preposition, and avoiding long strings of rhyming words. Sections (V) through (VIII) thus deal with several ways of generating material for the sermon.

Though this work essentially follows the successive steps of scholastic sermon structure, it is not so much concerned with teaching them in due order as with the procedures involved and with grammatical and logical relationships in them.

Edition: Delorme 1944.

Discussion: d'Avray 1978 (on the intended use of the wordlists in part VII); Briscoe 1992, pp. 43–5.

Citations from Delorme 1944 by page.

17 Jacobus de Fusignano (Fusignano)

OP, Roman province, fl. 1290s, died 1333.[16]

Libellus artis predicatorie compositus a fratre Iacobo Fusignani ordinis fratrum predicatorum, "Oro ut caritas uestra magis ac magis habundet ... Omni operi omnique actioni."

Caplan 115 (22 manuscripts, incunables). Charland 54–5.

16 Kaeppeli 1970, vol. 2, pp. 321–2.

Occurs with Predicacio and Quamvis in Oxford, University College, MS 36.

After applying the initial quotation of Philippians 1:9–10 ("I pray that your love may increase more and more") to the four (Aristotelian) causes and further to preaching (I), Jacobus turns to the preacher as the *causa efficiens instrumentalis*, whose thema should come exclusively from Scripture, while his supporting authorities may also be taken from authoritative doctors of the Church as well as from moral philosophers (II). Then Jacobus deals with the choice of the thema (III), which may be followed by a protheme and then a prayer (IV). This is expanded by various methods: by dealing with the entire gospel lection, by making immediately a distinction of a main term or notion from the thema, or by dividing the thema (V). In the last case, the parts of the division are to be developed further by subdivision or other techniques. Thus, the sermon is like a tree: it rises from its thema (the root) into a protheme (the trunk), then divides into parts (branches, *rami*), and these may divide further by subdivision or other procedures (twigs, *ramusculi*; VI). The twigs must then be developed with the help of twelve modes (VII), which are successively dealt with: using further biblical quotations that agree with the thema (VIII), discussing individual words (IX), interpreting a name and defining or describing a noun (X), using the fourfold sense of scripture (XI), using degrees of comparison and compound words (XII), synonyms (XIII), discussing the properties of things (XIV), exemplification with exempla, miracle stories, fables, and the like (XV), exploring the opposite of a word in the thema (XVI), dividing a whole into its parts (XVII), discussing the causes and effects of a vice or virtue (XVIII), and various processes of reasoning (XIX).

Edition and translation: Wenzel 2013b, pp. 3–95.

Discussion: Jennings 1989, pp. 100–1; Morenzoni 1997, pp. 285–7.

Citations from Wenzel 2013b by page (the Latin text, English translation on the next page).

18 Dic nobis (Dic)

Anonymous, perhaps by a Dominican, fourteenth century.

"*Dic nobis quid tibi videtur* … Reuerendi patres, ex quadruplici causa."

Not in Caplan or Charland. 1 manuscript (Padua, Biblioteca Antoniana, MS 515).

This sermon, preserved in a collection of sermons of English provenance, declares that its thema ("Tell us, what does it seem to you," Matthew 22:17) praises the art of sermon making (*ars sermocinandi*) for the four (Aristotelian) causes it contains. These are then developed, and the long part on the material cause forms a genuine *ars praedicandi*, in which the preacher deals with the thema, its introduction, a bridge passage, the division, subdivision, and confirmation. He ends the sermon with a combination of its parts. In all this, he again and again illustrates his points with material taken from his own thema, the initial quotation.

Edition: Wenzel 2008a.

Citations from Wenzel 2008a by page.

19 Quamvis de sermonibus (Quamvis)

Anonymous; the work has been attributed to Thomas Penketh, OESA (died 1487), but for several reasons the attribution is unconvincing. In Utrecht, University Library, MS 317, it is ascribed to an otherwise unknown English Dominican "Johannes de Gwidernia." Composed possibly before c. 1340. See Wenzel 2013b, pp. 102–3.

De sermonibus pertractandis vel eciam collacionibus. "Quamuis de sermonibus faciendis certa ars tradi non possit."

Caplan 144 and Caplan Suppl 144, listing a total of 3 manuscripts. Charland 90–1. Sharpe 674 ("Thomas Penketh") adds two more: Cambridge, University Library, MS Gg.6.20, an abbreviated copy; and Cambridge, Corpus Christi College, MS 423, pt. 2, in which the text of Quamvis is amalgamated with Predicacio and Alcok. A sixth copy is preserved in Utrecht, University Library, MS 317 (Caplan 78).

Occurs together with Hic and Vade in Lincoln, Cathedral Library, MS 234 and in London, BL, MS Additional 24361; with Waleys, Schale, and Circa in Cambridge, University Library, MS Gg.6.20; with Ad habendum in Utrecht, University Library, MS 317; in its amalgamated form together with Alcok in Cambridge, Corpus Christi College, MS 423; and in an abbreviated form together with Predicacio and Fusignano in Oxford, University College, MS 36.

The author at once announces three parts he will treat in this *notula*: (I) the introduction of the thema, (II) the division of the thema, and (III) the development of the members. The last is the longest section. It discusses (1) subdividing the members created in the division and developing them in different ways; and (2) adducing another authority for a proof text quoted in the division, subdividing it, and developing its members.

Edition and translation: Wenzel 2013b, pp. 97–143.

Citations from Wenzel 2013b by page (the Latin text, English translation on the next page).

20 *Ars copiosa sermonum* (Ars copiosa)

Anonymous.

Ars copiosa sermonum (colophon), "Ad euidenciam simplicium ut seipsos in collationibus ac sermonibus proficere ualeant."

Caplan Suppl b (2 mss, but see the next item; the full text is in Valencia, Cathedral Library, MS 184, ff. 14–29). Charland 96.

This long treatise begins with two "preambles," in which its author lists the authentic books of Holy Scripture and then describes the four senses of Scripture with rules. In the following introduction he distinguishes two kinds of preaching: (i) *ad placitum,* a free form as the preacher chooses, which can be "literal" (essentially following the gospel text) or "historical" (based on stories from the Fathers, examples, and fables); and (ii) *artificialis,* according to the rules of sermon technique, which can be the allegorical development of a biblical image (such as "city") or be based on nature, reason, and artifice. This last kind will be dealt with in the sections that follow.

After invoking Augustine, the author announces ten topics, from protheme to the final tying up. The actual development, however, shows some confusion and deals with: (I) the protheme; (II) the thema; (III) the bridge passage (*radix*); (IV) the division; (V) the subdivision; (VI) the subdistinction; (VII) *artificium,* i.e., a passage before and after a distinction which indicates the reason for a given proof text; (VIII) the confirmation (or proof text) for the parts of a division or distinction, always to be taken from Scripture; this part includes ways of development (distinction, digression, exemplification, reasoning, etc.); and (IX) tying up parts, including the sermon's conclusion.

The work frequently considers various possibilities, such as differences between preaching to the people and to the clergy. Further, the order in which it discusses sermon elements often deviates from what may be considered the standard treatment. Thus, it deals with the protheme before the thema, and in discussing the latter it begins with the demand to analyse the grammatical person used in the thema before giving the main requirements in choosing the thema. Here and elsewhere Ars copiosa seems to follow Rochelle.

Unedited.

Citations from Valencia, Cathedral Library, MS 184 by folio.

21 Ad erudicionem (Ad erudicionem)

Anonymous.

Caplan Suppl b (see the previous item; the unique copy is Cambridge, University Library, MS Ii.3.8, ff. 37–40v). Charland 96. For the manuscript see Wenzel 2005a, pp. 175–81.

An abbreviated version of Ars copiosa with some additional material. It begins with a preface that deals with different kinds of preaching (= Ars copiosa) and then announces seven "chapters." Of these only five are executed. They treat: (I) the thema (= Ars copiosa II); (II) the division (= Ars copiosa IV); (III) the distinction (= Ars copiosa V in part); (IV) the tying together (= Ars copiosa IX shortened); and (V) a brief paragraph on the likeness and difference between *sermo* and *collatio* (not in Ars copiosa). In general, Ad erudicionem is considerably less sophisticated than Ars copiosa, although here and there it adds some minor details.

Unedited.

Citations from Cambridge, University Library, MS Ii.3.8 by folio.

22 Thomas Waleys (Waleys)

OP, Oxford master, died 1350. See Sharpe 685–6 and Tugwell 2004.

De theoria sive arte praedicandi, "Reverendo in Christo patri ac domino Theobaldo de Ursinis ... Cum praedicationis officium sit potius angelicum quam humanum."

Caplan 32 (6 manuscripts). Charland 94–5.

Occurs with Thetford in Basel, Universitätsbibliothek, MS B.x.9; with Alcok in London, BL, MS Royal 8.E.xii; with Circa, an abbreviated version of Quamvis, and Schale in Cambridge, University Library, MS Gg.6.20; with two versions of Higden and Circa in Oxford, Bodleian Library, MS Bodley 5; and as an abridged version with Alcok in Oxford, Lincoln College, MS Lat. 101.

In the prologue the well-known English Dominican dedicates this long, comprehensive work to the archbishop of Palermo and declares that it is impossibile to deal with all forms and modes of preaching. He is aware of different ways of preaching used in the past but focuses on practices used by preachers *moderni temporis,* thus dealing with (I) rules (which are here and throughout the work called *documenta,* "topics of teaching") regarding the preacher: his attitude and disposition, clothing, gestures, speech habits, practising, etc.; (II) the thema; (III) the exhortation and prayer, which may be introduced in different ways including a protheme; (IV) digression, and various (historical) ways of developing the thema; (V) the introduction of the thema; (VI) the division, with differentiation between division, distinction, and taking up several items not derived by division or distinction; (VII) other features of the division, concerning sound and sense; (VIII) the order of development (*modus procedendi*) of the parts after the division; (IX) further considerations about the development (*dilatatio*): combining a string of authorities and other ways of expansion; these concern dealing with words – Waleys does not speak of *exempla* and pious stories – and are both rich and thoughtful: for instance, at one point Waleys ponders using different (Latin) translations of an original biblical authority in the same development (401).

The entire work is characterized by careful attention to minor matters and practical sense. For instance, after stating the general rule that the Sunday sermon should take its thema from the respective gospel lection, Waleys adds that if several sermons are given in the same place, or if the preacher gives several sermons in different places, he may choose a thema from outside the given lection (342). In addition, Waleys often speaks in his own person. For example, in section (IX) he adds modes of dilation that "occurred" to him, granting that there may be many others that did not (402). Elsewhere he reports what he had witnessed (e.g., 333) or criticizes certain practices (343, 356, etc.). In general, his style is leisurely, and he furnishes many, often lengthy, illustrations. All this forms only the first part of Waleys's treatise, in which he several times refers to a second and third part that furnish sample sermons *de tempore* and, apparently, *de sanctis,* in order to illustrate how to handle the division and its members.

Edited: Charland 328–403 (only part 1!).

Translation: Grosser 1949. Camargo 2010 (translation of chap. 1, on the quality of the preacher).
Discussion: Murphy 1974, pp. 333–4; Roth 1956, pp. 107–17; Briscoe 1992, pp. 40–2.
Citations from Charland by page.

23 Ranulph Higden (Higden)

OSB, St Werburgh Abbey, Chester; died 1364. See Taylor 2004.
Ars componendi sermones or *De arte praedicandi*, "Circa sermones artificialiter faciendos … Rectitudo intencionis."
Caplan 156 (4 mss, one containing two copies of the work). Charland 76.
Occurs (two copies) with Waleys and Circa in Oxford, Bodleian Library, MS Bodley 5.

This fairly long work by an English Benedictine well known for his world history (*Polychronicon*) and a pastoral manual (*Speculum curatorum*) is the product of compiling material from a number of sources, mostly Basevorn, Waleys, Wales, and Ps.-Bonaventure, and apparently also Quamvis.[17] It begins with a short section of general considerations concerning the parts of a sermon, which may or may not have been part of Higden's original version. This is followed by a proper *prefacio* ("Ad preeminentem huius artis laudem") that declares the author's wish to present what he has gleaned from various authors "ad erudicionem simplicium." Higden quotes with slight changes the definitions of *predicacio* by John of Wales and by Basevorn, though without mentioning their names.[18] After quickly specifying the four causes of preaching, he lists twenty chapters (II–XXI in the edition), in which he

17 The sources are indicated in Jennings 1991, pp. 73–80. For material borrowed from Quamvis see Wenzel 2013b, pp. 251–5.

18 "Secundum quosdam predicacio est invocato dei auxilio thema proponere, propositum dividere, divisum subdividere, auctoritates confirmantes cum racionibus et exemplis adducere, et adductas explanare ad divini cultus ampliacionem, ecclesie militantis illustracionem, humani affectus erga deum inflamacionem; vel secundum alios predicacio est publica persuasio debitis loco et tempore pluribus facta ad salutem promerendam" (5).

discusses several qualities that a preacher must have (II–V) and then the parts of a scholastic sermon: thema (VI–X), protheme (XI), initial prayer (XII), capturing the audience's attention (XIII), introduction of the thema (XIV), division (XV–XVI, with confirmation), development (XVII–XX), and coloration, i.e., end rhyme and *cursus* or *cadentia* (XXI). Most of the chapters are relatively short, but XI, XIV–XVI, XIX, and XX contain longer expositions that parallel the treatments of these topics in other *artes*. Of special interest is his constant awareness of themata of a single word (24, 41–3, etc.).

Though Higden took virtually all his material from a number of unacknowledged sources, he combined it in an intelligent and orderly way, thus avoiding for example the longueurs and structural problems of Basevorn. An immediately evident aspect of his orderly mind is his custom of beginning the treatment of a given topic with stating its parts and then discussing them seriatim.

Edition: Jennings 1991.

Translation: Jennings and Wilson 2003.

Discussion: Murphy 1974, pp. 335–6; Jennings 1978 and Jennings 1991, pp. xxxv–xlvii and 73–80 (outline and sources); the outline again in Jennings 2006, pp. 323–4.

Citations from Jennings 1991 by page.

24 Thomas de Tuderto (or of Todi) (Tuderto)

OSA, c. 1380.

Ars sermocinandi ac collationes faciendi, "Venerabilibus ac reverendis dominisque ... Ars sermocinandi ac etiam faciendi collationes prima facie dividitur in septem partes ..."

Caplan 16 and Caplan Suppl 16, etc. Charland 92–3 (20 mss).

Occurs with Eiximenes and Alprão in Cracow, Biblioteka Jagiellońska, MS 471.

The work immediately announces seven chapters (*particulae*), which are then developed at some length:

(I) The division of the thema (1–17).
(II) Subdivision (17–22).
(III) Confirmation of the parts, here called *probatio* (22–8).

(IV) Development of the parts, here called *prolixitas* and *multiplicatio* (29–37).
(V) The *ordinatio* of a sermon and of a *collatio*. Thomas here lists eight[19] parts: *thematis propositio, Virginis salutatio, thematis introductio, thematis divisio, divisionum subdivisio, divisionum et subdivisionum probatio, rhythorum ordinatio,* and *sermonis conclusio.* These, he says, have already been treated, or will be treated in following *particulae*, or are treated in this *particula V* (37–41).
(VI) The introduction of the thema (41–68).
(VII) The use of rhymes (68–81).

Though Thomas's order of these chapters is curious – in that one would expect (V) and (VI) to precede (I) – they contain and deal with all the standard elements of scholastic sermon structure. Each chapter presents several modes and ample illustrations. Given this curious, confusing structure, I have added, above, the page numbers to the chapter numbers as in the edited text.

Edition: Babcock 1941; presented as a "transliteration" from only one manuscript (with "restored" classical spellings), containing a large number of textual puzzles.

Discussion: Murphy 1974, pp. 339–40.

Citations from Babcock 1941 by page.

25 Henry of Hesse (Hesse)

The author mentioned in the work's title may be Heinrich von Langenstein (1325–97), theologian and rector of the University of Vienna.

Tractatulus eximii doctoris Henrici de Hassia de arte praedicandi valde utilis, "Ars predicandi est scientia docens de aliquo aliquid dicere."

19 Babcock's *semptempliciter ordinatur sermo sive collatio* should probably read *similiter* ... (37). For the collation, Thomas only specifies that it should have a *verbum perambulum* before the thema (40, which should probably read *preambulum*), giving two examples of his own.

Caplan 14 and Caplan Suppl 14 and others. Charland 43–4. The relationships among the extant copies in the many manuscripts and incunabula, as well as between this and similar anomyous treatises, are very confusing.

The work begins with the four senses of Scripture linked, respectively, to the gospel, Gregory, Ambrose, and Augustine. It then discusses four modes of preaching:

(1) *antiquissimus* or *postillatio,* used by Christ and the Church Fathers (literal or moral interpretation of Scripture);
(2) *modernus,* with thema, protheme, division, and subdivision as essential parts;
(3) *antiquus,* used after the Fathers and before the *modernus,* with thema, protheme, distinction, and subdistinction;
(4) *subalternus,* a mixture of *antiquus* and *modernus,* with division, subdivision, distinction, and subdistinction. This section also contains rules about elocution, dilatation, and conclusion.

The style of this treatise in general is rather short and lapidary, leaving much of its teaching opaque. Modes 2–4 are dealt with at some length and with brief examples. At the end the author adds a short list of preaching aids: biblical concordances, *Decretum, Lumen animae,* a book of similitudes, *Compendium theologicae veritatis,* and the *Summae* of Thomas Aquinas. The preponderance of Dominican works here suggests that the treatise is of Dominican authorship (cf. Caplan 1933, pp. 360–1).

Edition and translation Caplan 1933.
Citations from Caplan 1933 by page.

26 Geoffrey Schale (Schale)

OSA, from Ireland, preached at Council of Constance, probably in 1417; died in or shortly after 1421.

"Fecunda gracia Saluatoris ... In principio enim cuiuslibet artificalis sermonis."

Caplan Suppl 17a (2 mss). Charland 37. Sharpe 128.

Occurs with Waleys, Circa, and the abbreviated version of Quamvis in Cambridge, University Library, MS Gg.6.20.

A brief treatment of the main features of the sermon in sequence: thema, *antethema* with prayer, introduction to the thema, division (called the sermon's *fundamentum*), distinction, development (*prosecutio*) by various means, and conclusion. The section on development contains longer illustrations that amount to virtually an entire sermon. Throughout, the treatise uses some material from Quamvis. It ends with the author naming himself and asking for the reader's prayer.

Unedited.

Discussion: Zumkeller 1970, pp. 6–7 (life and his sermon); Wenzel 2013b, pp. 246–8.

Citations from Cambridge, University Library, MS Gg.6.20 by folio.

27 Omnis rei inicio (Omnis)

Anonymous, probably by a Franciscan author. The explicit calls it *ars sermocinandi utilis, breuis et ualde bona pro introducendis rudibus in ea.*

"Omnis res inicio, medio et fine metitur."

Not in Caplan or Charland. See Morenzoni 2006 (1 ms).

Occurs with another *ars* attributed to Nicholas of Oresme (died 1382) in the unique manuscript (Paris, Bibliothèque Nationale, MS Lat. 7371).

Beginning with a quote from Aristotle,[20] the treatise declares that, like everything else, a sermon must have a beginning, middle, and end. These are (I) the thema, which must have six qualities. It must then be applied to the intention of the sermon by means of an introduction, which can be made in eight ways. (II) The division. A lengthy definition is given, whose parts are explained and illustrated. To it are added its exposition (i.e., a second division), embellishment (*ornatus*, actually a further extension), adaptation (which establishes the connection between a member of the division and its corresponding term in the thema), and confirmation (*probatio*). (III) The development (*dilatio* or *prosecutio*), including continuous division or subdivision with confirmation; distinction; and other methods. For illustration a hypothetical sermon in praise of "beatus Franciscus" is used.

20 Aristotle, *De coelo*, 1.1.268a.10–15, cited by Aquinas, *Summa theologiae* III.53.2, in Thomas Aquinas, *Summa theologiae*, ed. Petrus Caramello, 4 vols (Turin, 1948), 4:332.

Though this treatise aims at introducing the uninformed (*rudes*) to the art of preaching, it stands out by its logical approach, especially by giving long and careful definitions of several key terms (*divisio, distinctio, descriptio*) and explaining their terms.

Edition and discussion: Morenzoni 2006.

Citations from Morenzoni 2006 by page.

28 Francesc Eiximenes (Eiximenes)

OFM, of the Barcelona province, 1340–1409.

Modus sermocinandi or *Ars predicandi populo,* "Jhesus Christus tocius nature pastor ... Circa finem predicacionis."

Caplan 84 and Caplan Suppl 84 (and 73; three mss, one of which names Eiximenes in its title). Charland 35–6.

Occurs with Rochelle, Wales, Lull, and another *ars praedicandi* in Vatican Library, MS Ottoboni 396; and with Tuderto and Alprão in Cracow, Biblioteca Jagiellońska, MS 471.

The prologue to this long work announces, with an abundance of adjectives in the superlative, four *capitula,* which are the four (Aristotelian) causes of preaching. Three of them are then dealt with at some length: chapter I, on *causa finalis,* covers three possible ends of preaching, of which the third, the preacher's own merit, is sharply criticized – a stance that runs through the entire treatise. Chapter II, on *causa efficiens,* indicates the qualities a good preacher must have. Chapter III, on *causa formalis,* then treats the form of preaching. This is the longest part of the work. It discusses seven qualities of good preaching or of a good sermon: brevity, fervour, breadth, devotion, moral teaching, prudence, and order (*ordinatio*), and includes much good advice, such as what facial expressions and gestures the preacher should and should not use, or that after his sermon he should wait some time before chatting with his listeners, or how he should act if he is praised for his preaching. The final point of this chapter, on *ordinatio,* again covers several large topics: how to find matter for one's sermon (corresponding to *inventio* of classical rhetoric – this may be the *causa materialis* announced earlier but not treated in a separate part); the use of memory (which in fact is a little *ars memoriae*); and how to compose a sermon in an orderly fashion. In the latter section (331–9) Eiximenes discusses older and modern modes of preaching, and at last focuses on what he considers the three main parts of the modern sermon: choosing a thema, introducing it, and dividing it, with further expansion (there is some confusion of terms in this section). All this is developed at some length, with several points and occasional critiques. There is no separate chapter on the *causa materialis*; the discussion of the preacher's subject matter may already have been included in chapter III. Instead, Eiximenes adds "some counsels that the holy father Abbas Efrem put down in his *Doctrina*," which concern mostly the preacher's behavior. In chapter III he mentions sermons that are to be added "below" (314, 315, 330), but there are none in the edition.

Edition: Barcelona 1936.

Discussion: Barraque 2008 (biography, pp. 532–4); Briscoe 1992, pp. 45–7; Rivers 1999 (summary of the work, discussion of *ars memoriae*); Rivers 2010, pp. 161–79 and passim.

Citations from Barcelona 1936 by page.

29 Alfonso d'Alprão (Alprão)

OFM, in Spain, inquisitor in Portugal in 1412.

Ars praedicandi, conferendi, collationandi, arengandi, secundum multiplicem modum, etc. (Var. *Tractatus et ars de modo praedicandi*), "Dividitur iste tractatus in duas partes, scilicet in prologum et processum." Apparently written at Bologna in 1397.

Caplan 72 and Caplan Suppl 72 (2 mss, with author's name). Charland 25.

Occurs with Tuderto and Eiximenes in Cracow, Biblioteka Jagiellońska, MS 471.

Of the two principal parts announced in the first sentence, only the first, called *prologus*, is extant. It has three sections: (I) the introduction of the thema, (II) the division, and (III) the distinction of the parts. In (I) Alprão includes a short discussion of the thema and then lists ten ways of introducing it: syllogism, enthymeme, induction, exemplum, quoting a saintly author (*originale*), quoting a philosopher, division, distinction, a biblical figure or narrative, and a question. These are dealt with and exemplified by being applied to one and the same thema used for illustration throughout the treatise (*In capite eius corona*, "On her head a crown," Revelation 12:1), and they form long sections, especially the development of an authority by means of a syllogism. The procedures here described can in fact be valid for the development of an authority anywhere in the sermon, including the sermon's main development. What Alprão proposes in (I) amounts to a very lengthy "introduction" of the thema, and he acknowledges this by saying that "the introduction alone could suffice for the sermon, as it is done nowadays" (quod sola introductio sufficiat pro sermone, ut tempore fit moderno, 272). Parts (II) and (III) then are much shorter.

Edition and discussion: Hauf 1979 (with consideration of similar treatments in other *artes*).

Citations from Hauf 1979 by page.

30 Antoninus of Florence (Antoninus)

Saint, OP, archbishop of Florence, 1389–1459.

Caplan 216. Charland 26.

The encyclopedic *Summa theologica* of St Antoninus includes a section on the office of preaching, in part III, title 18, where its author discusses the office and qualities of preachers (chapter III), their defects (ch. IV), sermon form (*De forma predicacionis,* chapter V), and modes of amplification (chapter VI). In the same chapter VI he adds "books that, after the Bible, are superior to others for the expansion of the sermon," which eventually leads him to list the authentic books of the New and Old Tetament, apocrypha, and others, all this with references to canon law. In chapter V, after declaring that "no definite mode can be found that has been handed on by the saints and must be followed of necessity," Antoninus details at some length seven ways in which a preacher can proceed, namely by (1) exposition of the gospel, as used in the homilies of the *antiqui* (Gregory, Augustine, Chrysostom); (2) choosing a scriptural passage as the thema and dividing it (which Antoninus calls *modus magistralis* and *magis scientificus,* practiced by Aquinas, Bonaventure, Bernardino, and others); (3) preaching with the help of distinctions, as practised by Bernard, Gregory, and Cassian, for which the *Distinctiones Mauricii* are helpful; (4) detailing effects, causes, conditions, degrees, species, properties of things, or names – Antoninus appears to have been very fond of enumeration, here and throughout his section on sermon form; (5) quoting a proof text from the Psalms or any other biblical book after reciting the gospel or epistle (which may be recited *in toto*) and dividing or applying it to the thema; (6) using interpretation, etymology, or explanation of a name in the thema; and (7) expanding on the letters of a word contained in the thema (i.e., acrostic or *excoriatio*).[21] Chapter VI then deals with "dilating one's matter" and likewise explains a number of techniques: (1) adducing another authority from Scripture, canon law, a saintly doctor, or a pagan philosopher; (2) reasoning; (3) definition or description; (4) etymology; (5) a *figura* from Scripture; (6) similitudes from nature; (7) examples from Schripture or elsewhere; (8) praising or reprimanding. Chapters V and VI seem to some extent to overlap, but Antoninus treats logically distinct subjects: the sermon as a whole (chapter V) and ways of expansion (chapter VI).

The various forms and methods are illustrated with many examples, often by taking one thema for a *de tempore* sermon and another for a saint's sermon. In all cases, the elements of a method are completely developed, with proof texts, leading to lengthy illustrations. Antoninus also refers to such near contemporary preachers as Bernardino, Jacobus de Voragine, and Johannes de San Gemigniano.

Printed edition: Antoninus 1486.

Discussion: Howard 1995; Briscoe 1992, pp. 48–50.

Citations from Antoninus 1486, from the copy in the Rare Book Room at the University of North Carolina at Chapel Hill. References are to chapters V and VI, with subsections (in the edition the latter marked as paragraphs).

31 Simon Alcok (Alcok)

Secular Oxford master, fl. 1420s, died 1459. See Rex 2004.

Tractatus de modo dividendi thema pro materia dilatanda ... "Ad, quare, per, propter ... In predictis versibus continentur dictiones."

Caplan 8 and 9. Charland 83–4. Boynton 1941 lists 7 mss and 1 (textually poor) incunable (c. 1480), to which add Dublin, Trinity College Library, MS 424. Sharpe p. 608 is inaccurate, as is Rex.

Occurs with Waleys in London, BL, MS Royal 8.E.xii; and with the amalgamated version of Quamvis as well as some material from Ps.-Bonaventure in Cambridge, Corpus Christi College, MS 423.

The work begins with eight hexameters that list the initial words of 45 ways of dividing the thema and in fact any biblical authority at any

21 For *excoriatio*, see below, p. 81.

place in the sermon, thereby generating matter for the sermon's development. Thus, *Ad* signals the effect or aim of what the thema speaks of; *Quare* asks why something is declared in the thema; *Per*, through what this is done, and so forth. For instance, the thema *Te salvum fecit* can be divided into *ad tui liberacionem*, or *ut te a baratro liberaret*, or *per sanguinis effusionem*, and so on. These ways include more general procedures, such as definition or simple *postillatio*.

Edition: Boynton 1941.

Citations from Boynton 1941 by page.

32 Martin of Cordoba (Cordoba)

OESA, lector at Salamanca 1420, died 1476.

Ars praedicandi, "Huius codicelli breuitas precepta novellis dabit predicatoribus."

Caplan 192 (1 ms). Charland 70.

The prologue declares that this work is humble yet gathers valuable basic advice on sermon making for young (*novellis*) preachers, in eight parts: (I) definition of sermon as "an informative speech coming from the mouth of a preacher and instructing the faithful what to do, what to keep from, what to fear, and what to hope for," whose parts are then explained in terms of the four (Aristotelian) causes of preaching;[22] (II) the thema, similarly defined, with rules; in the sermon it may be followed by a protheme or exordium; (III) introduction of the thema, with ten modes; (IV) division, with ten rules; (V) development of the parts (*prosecutio*) and confirmation (*probatio*); (VI) use of a biblical *figura*; (VII) dilatation of the sermon in particular; the edited text speaks of fourteen modes but then gives only ten, which are the same (with the same illustrations) as those in Ad habendum (see above, p. 14); (VIII) various ways of explaining Scripture: the four senses, name etymology, etc. The treatise thus does not develop the parts of a scholastic sermon in sequence but discusses major techniques that may be used in several places.

---

22 "Sermo est oratio informatiua ex ore predicatoris emissa, ut instruat fideles quid credere, quid agere, quid cauere, quid timere, quid sperare debeant. Unde notandum quod iuxta definitionem tanguntur quattuor cause ipsius sermonis" (331–2).

Edition: Rubió 1959; the edited text is quite poor, containing a number of grammatically erroneous and suspect readings.
Discussion: Goldberg 1974 (on life and works, pp. 19, 60–1).
Citations from Rubió 1959 by page.

33 Christian Borgsleben (Borgsleben)

OFM, theologian at Leipzig and Erfurt, died after 1484.
Ars predicandi, "Cum in his temporibus plures sint universitates."
Caplan Suppl 155a (1 ms; to which add Leipzig, Universitätsbibliothek, MS 616, which mentions Borgsleben in its title and *explicit*; see Buchwald 1921). Charland 33.
Occurs in the Leipzig manuscript with material from other *artes praedicandi.*

A short and fairly simple treatise giving practical advice (minimam et quasi nullam artem) without systematically treating scholastic sermon structure. Its short preface speaks of the training of young preachers at Erfurt and the author's intention to provide students sent there with the technique of making *collationes* and *sermones*, in four parts: (I) the thema; (II) the division with concording proof texts; (III) two extended examples of collations; (IV) how to introduce a sermon (or more properly, the thema) to the people, in the vernacular. He considers three ways and then explains and illustrates them: (a) by speaking of the opposite to a term in the thema; (b) by analysing and speaking about the meaning of a term in the thema, which can be illustrated with authorities from Scripture or other writers, examples, etc.; (c) by citing an authority (non-biblical) that contains a division or distinction. All this is illustrated with *exempla multum puerilia*; for more "polished" examples Borgsleben refers by name to (apparently) Bertrandus de Turri, OFM, and Petrus Niger, OP.

Edition: Buchwald 1921.
Citations from Buchwald 1921 by page.

34 Hic docet (Hic)

Anonymous.
"Hic docet Augustinus 4 *De doctrina Christi*: Omnis tradicio ... Et quia in hiis duobus."

Not in Caplan or Charland. Preserved in two mss, where it immediately follows Quamvis: Lincoln, Cathedral Library, MS 234, and London, BL, Additional MS 24361.

After the initial reference to St Augustine and a general distinction between *sermo* and *collatio*, the author announces that he will deal with four main features of a *collatio*: (I) the introduction of the thema, in a general way; (II) its division; (III) its subdivision; and (IV) the use of proof texts for confirmation. After discussing these, he adds another section (V), in which he deals with some specific differences between a *sermo* and a *collatio*. Illustrations are very sparse.

Edition and translation: Wenzel 2013b, pp. 145–61.

Citations from Wenzel 2013b by page (the Latin text, English translation on the next page).

35 Vade in domum tuam (Vade)

Anonymous.

"*Vade in domum tuam*. Secundum Magistrum *Historiarum* in principio."

Not in Caplan. Cf. Charland 106. In 2 manuscripts (Lincoln, Cathedral Library, MS 234, ff. 179–82v; and London, BL, MS Additional 24361, ff. 60–3), where it follows after Quamvis and Hic; in a third manuscript, Wolfenbüttel, Herzog August Bibliothek, MS 4047, ff. 1–16, the text appears amalgamated with material from other *artes* and rearranged; see Wenzel 2013b, p. 164.

Occurs with Quamvis and Hic (see above).

Using the initial quotation of Matthew 9:6 ("Go into your house"), the unknown author compares the parts of a house to the six parts of a sermon, which he then deals with in sequence: (I) foundation = the thema; (II) wall = the introduction of the thema; (III) door, with threshold, opening, and lock = the *pedis positio* (see below, p. 61), division of the thema, announcement or explanation of the parts, and confirmation; (IV–V) windows with panes = the subdivision or distinction; (VI) roof = the final tying together. The parts are briefly illustrated with examples that are usually based on the work's initial quotation.

Edition and translation: Wenzel 2013b, pp. 163–87.

Citations from Wenzel 2013b by page (the Latin text, English translation on the next page).

36 Circa artem (Circa)

Anonymous, fifteenth century, probably from England.
Ars faciendi sermonem, "Circa artem faciendi sermonem siue collacionem."
Caplan 23 and Caplan Suppl 23 (1 ms). Charland 97 adds a second ms with variant incipit. For the latter, see Jennings 1991, pp. xlii–xliii.
Occurs with Waleys, Quamvis, and Schale in Cambridge, University Library, MS Gg.6.20; and with Waleys and two versions of Higden in Oxford, Bodleian Library, MS Bodley 5.

The relatively short treatise begins at once with advice on choosing a thema and distinguishing between the different grammatical moods it can have: indicative, imperative, or optative – an emphasis that runs throughout the work. It then prescribes how to handle them (*probari*) by illustrating several ways of introducing the thema. Next it deals with the division, which is to be introduced with a bridge passage (*pes*), and then discusses such features as *claves, sufficientia, conveniencia,* and the *sensus moralis*. The following section deals with proof texts for the parts and how one can combine the parts. The final section discusses how a sermon differs from a collation, again paying attention to the different grammatical moods of the thema. The densely logical style of the work makes the exposition occasionally hard to follow, especially in light of evident scribal errors, but one's understanding is much helped by the illustrations provided.

Unedited.
Citations from Cambridge, University Library, MS Gg.6.20 by folio.

37 In accepcione thematis (In accepcione)

Anonymous. Fifteenth century.
De modo sermozinandi, "In accepcione thematis primo cauendum est."
Caplan 57 (1 ms). Charland 100. A second manuscript is noted in Wenzel 1994, p. 47 (Arras, Bibliothèque de la Ville, MS 184 [254], ff. 30va–31rb), which is perhaps a shorter or abbreviated version.
Occurs with another *ars* (Caplan 135) in Cambridge, Gonville and Caius College, MS 240.

This treatise of only one folio (in the Arras manuscript) clearly demonstrates the main steps or features of the scholastic sermon as taught in the later Middle Ages: thema (how to choose it), *antethema* leading to prayer, resumption of thema, introduction of thema, division with confirmation, development (*prosecucio*), and conclusion. These are briefly explained and illustrated with reference to the thema *Rex tuus venit* ("Your king is coming," Matthew 21:5).

Unedited.

Citations from Arras, Bibliothèque de la Ville, MS 184 (254) by folio.

38 Nota pro arte (Nota)

Anonymous, perhaps Franciscan. The work was probably added in the fifteenth century on blank sheets in an otherwise fourteenth-century manuscript.

"Nota pro arte faciendi collaciones et sermones."

Caplan 89 (1 ms). Charland 102.

The poorly preserved text likens a collation or sermon to a tree, with the following parts: its root (*radix*) is the thema; its trunk (*stips*) the bridge passage (*pedis posicio*) leading to the division; its branches (*rami*) form the division; its leaves (*folia*) are embellishments; and its fruit (*fructus*) is the edification of the audience and the praise of God and his saints. This is followed by a section discussing how the preacher, here always called *conferens* (i.e., one who gives a *collatio*), may expand a collation into a sermon by various processes of dilatation, such as subdivision, taking the opposite to what the text has stated, and others. All this is illustrated with examples for a putative sermon *Vidit et sequebatur* ("He saw and followed," Luke 18:43 and Mark 10:52). An interesting feature is the author's citing Aristotle and an unnamed *commentator* on making a division (*Metaphysics* 7.12).

Unedited.

Citations from Lincoln, Cathedral Library, MS 227 by folio.

39 Si vis sermonem (Si vis)

Anonymous, probably fifteenth century.

[*Tractatus de arte predicandi.*] "Si vis sermon ex arte conficere."

Caplan 170 (1 ms). Charland p. 105.

This short but curious treatise tells its readers to choose a convenient thema, divide it into two or three parts and subdivide these parts into, again, two or three parts, which will then serve as the principal parts of the sermon. Each of the latter is to be developed "in hora pronunctiationis" (i.e., during the delivery) in four ways: by "rhetorical argumentation" (i.e., presenting the subject matter), confirmation, confutation, and a conclusion. These four ways are defined, and the author shows that each can (or should?) be done in different forms. If a preacher lacks experience and knowledge, he should jot down relevant points and commit them to memory. And the author goes once more through the four ways, with further advice. The importance of this otherwise very slight treatise lies in its use of key terms from classical rhetoric: *argumentum* (for *narratio*), *confirmatio*, *confutatio*, and *conclusio*; see section 5 above on Chobham. But notice that the date of its composition is uncertain.

Edition: Evans 1980.

Citations from Evans 1980 by page.

40 Ps.-Aquinas (Ps.-Aquinas)

Anonymous, sometimes acribed to Thomas Aquinas.

Tractatulus [var. *Tractatus*] *solemnis de arte et vero modo predicandi*, "Communicaturus meis desiderantibus hoc quod de modo predicandi ad populos."

Caplan 217. Charland 85–8 (about a dozen mss, with variants; and incunable editions).

The anonymous author introduces his "little compendium, laboriously compiled from various books of holy doctors" by quoting several Church Fathers (including William of Auvergne) that the effective preaching of the word of God requires art. He then speaks of three kinds of preaching: oral, in writing, and in one's actions. Next he defines the first kind of preaching[23] and elaborates the terms of his definition. He mentions the efficient cause of preaching but not the other three. A

23 Using the definition given by Alan: "Manifesta publica instructio, fidei et morum hominum informationem deseruiens, ex rationum semita et auctoritatum fonte procedens" (3ra): see section 3.

paragraph details that the preacher should adapt his gestures and voice to the mood of the (biblical) words he pronounces. Then he turns to the parts of a sermon, which are four: thema, protheme (called *prelocutio*), division or distinction, and subdivision or subdistinction. These are somewhat developed and include a number of failings in preaching, such as ignorance, a boring delivery, pointing one's fingers, and so on. Eventually he continues that to the four parts must be added the development (*prolongatio*) of each part of the sermon, and he discusses, at greater length and with illustrations, nine modes of expansion. This is followed by twelve warnings (*cautele*): to preach with reverence, not to discuss controversial matters (*dubia*), not to drop one's voice at the end of a sentence, etc. After the work comes to an end, the compiler continues with likening the sermon to a tree, with root, trunk, and branches, and then explains three kinds of preaching (*triplex modus predicandi*): the *modus antiquus*, corresponding to the homiletic style of Gregory and the Fathers; preaching with distinctions; and the kind he had described earlier (i.e., the modern or scholastic sermon). An actual picture of a tree may have illustrated this sermon structure (though not printed in all incunables), which apparently had a number of leaves (?) inscribed with letters corresponding to various modes of expansion, for which the writer furnishes proof texts.

The treatise is indeed an abridged compilation from several works, whose seams often show. For instance, it deals with the twofold efficient cause (cf. Fusignano) but omits the other three causes that are often discussed in these treatises. Other material from Fusignano appears throughout, as do snatches from Ad habendum and Auvergne.

Printed edition: Ps.-Aquinas 1483.

Translation: Caplan 1925 (the tree diagram is reproduced in the reprint).

Discussion: Murphy 1974, pp. 338–9; Roth 1956, pp. 140–6.

Citations from Ps.-Aquinas 1483 by folio.

41 *Exercitacio in collacionibus* (Exercitacio)

Anonymous, perhaps by a Franciscan (the text illustrates one point with a sermon *de beato Francisco*).

Exercitacio in collacionibus (colophon), "Si quis wlt excercitari in collacionibus, per octo sequencia diligenter considerata poterit in eis aliqualiter manuduci."

Caplan 169 and Caplan Suppl 169 (1 ms). Charland 105.

Occurs with In predicatore and Rochelle (incomplete) in London, BL, MS Arundel 275, ff. 86rb–89vb.

Eight parts give instruction on how to construct a *collatio*. These are first listed and then discussed: (I) the meaning of *collatio*; (II) qualities of the thema; (III) adapting the thema to the intended purpose by analysing it and establishing a *proemium* or *prologus* (equivalent to what will be called the bridge passage in section 45-e, below); (IV) dividing the thema; (V) additional rules about the division, its members, and distinction; (VI) further rules about division/subdivision and the number of members; (VII) the (rational) order of the terms in the thema and divisions and their connections; (VIII) confirmation and concordance.

A stylistic curiosity of this treatise is its speaking of the preacher as *homo*. Many illustrations are related to the thema *Redde quod debes*.

Unedited.

Citations from London, BL, MS Arundel 275 by folio.

42 In predicatore (In predicatore)

Anonymous.

"In predicatore debent esse vita, sapiencia vel sciencia, et eloquencia."

Caplan 68 (the reading should be *predicatore*). Charland 101.

Occurs with Rochelle (imperfect) and Exercitacio in London, BL, MS Arundel 275, ff. 81vb–83rb, a fourteenth-century manuscript from Germany containing material of use to preachers, including a sermon on St Francis and the fables by Odo of Cheriton (see Herbert 1910, pp. 46–9).

After briefly describing the required qualities of a preacher, the author distinguishes "fruitful but dangerous preaching" (i.e., that of *questionarii*, "pardoners") from "fruitful and sane" preaching. He then further distinguishes between various kinds of preaching:

1. By exposition (*expositorius*):
   a) *vagus*, "wandering," that is, not sticking to a specific thema, as practised by Augustine, Ambrose, Jerome, etc.
   b) limited, namely to a specific thema, whether the preacher starts with it and goes on to other authorities, or starts with it,

explains all its parts, and in the end returns to it; as did Gregory and the ancient homiletic style.

2. By definition (*diffinitorius*): taking one word from the thema, giving its definition, and then elaborating the parts of the definition.
3. By division (*diuisiuus*): dividing a thema and developing its parts; used by most modern preachers. This third mode is discussed with further divisions and subdivisions, so that the gist of this treatise concerns describing and giving advice on the *divisio* of the scholastic sermon.

The distinction of various kinds of preaching offered here is unique among the treatises analysed, whether it was original with its anonymous author or derived from elsewhere, although the difference between the second and the third kind is realized by some *artes* when dealing with *distinctio* vs. *divisio*. Equally interesting is the author's extended concern with handling comparisons. For example: if in preaching on the name "Mary" one says that "in Scripture Mary is compared to a fountain because of her purity," the comparison is (logically) fitting. But if one were to preach on "Who is she that rises in the desert like a pillar of smoke?" and applies this verse to Mary by comparing her to different things that rise, such as a wellspring, the dawn, fire, and so on, the preacher must not say "Mary rises like a wellspring through [her] purity" because this statement is (logical) nonsense. Instead, the preacher should express the *tertium comparationis*, such as "As a wellspring rises because of the abundance of water in the ground, so the Blessed Virgin rises like a wellspring because of the richness of grace given to her" (82va–b). After presenting this illustration, the author continues: "Someone might say to me, 'This way of preaching was not used by holy preachers,'" to which he replies that nowadays many things are clear (*plana*) which to the ancients were not so.

Unedited.

Citations from London, BL, MS Arundel 275 by folio.

43 Ramon Lull (Lull)

A lay theologian (1232–1316), born of a wealthy Catalan family on Majorca and devoting his later life to composing works of logic, philosophy, and various branches of theology with the aim of converting Jews and Muslims rationally to the Christian faith. He travelled widely in southern Europe and the Mediterranean, was close to the Franciscans, and late in life became a member of the Franciscan Third Order. Though he knew Latin and Arabic, most of his many works (over 260) were probably written in Catalan and then translated into Latin.

Liber de praedicatione, "Deus gloriosissime ... Quoniam praedicatio est officium altissimum" (and variants). This is his main work on preaching; other works on preaching and on rhetoric are of little relevance to sermon structure.

Not in Caplan. Only mentioned in Charland 19. For manuscripts, see the edition listed below, to which should be added Vatican Library, MS Ottoboni 396.

Occurs with Wales, Eiximenes, and others in MS Ottoboni 396.

In his main work, *Ars generalis* (developed through several stages), Lull devised a logical system that would allow the reader to find the principles and relations underlying all things in the universe and by combining them to demonstrate the truth. This system is quite idiosyncratic and stands outside contemporary scholasticism. For instance, since the main categories of his system occur in groups of nine (labelled B–K), Lull lists not seven but nine vices (the seven deadly sins plus *mendacium* and *inconstantia*). Lull then applied the principles of his *Art* to various branches of learning, including rhetoric and preaching. The *Liber de praedicatione*, written at Montpellier in 1304, has two main parts. In the first Lull shows largely how the preacher, here called *sermocinator*, can find matter for his preaching about God, the universe, vices and virtues, and so on. The second part (II.A.1–9) speaks of "nine conditions" which the preacher follows in his work.

These are (in Lull's terms) *expositio, divisio, ordinatio, investigatio, probatio, comparatio, multiplicatio, ornatio,* and *deprecatio*. It is obvious that Lull was familiar with contemporary *artes praedicandi*, since he uses a number of key terms as well as major concerns. But he does so in a very curious way. For example, in the section on *ordinatio* he speaks of (1) the protheme, here called *introitus sermonis*; (2) the place (*locus*) of preaching, which includes not only the place where one is to preach but also the nature of his audience and what, in his sermon, he should put in the first place, the middle, and the end; (3) the time of preaching and length of the sermon; and (4) the preacher's *honestas*, i.e., his virtuous way of life. I have included references to Lull where he uses the respective technical terms, but the reader should keep in mind that in Lull's system these may occupy very different places. In a final section (II.B) Lull offers one hundred sermons, for the Church year, the saints, and the dead. Though these are intended as models that show how to apply the principles of his Art, they are not "model sermons" in the normal sense, insofar as Lull intrudes again and again with advice to the preacher.

Edition: Lull 1961.

Discussion: In Lull 1961 the editor, Soria Flores, discusses Lull's teaching on sermon structure as it appears in this work (pp. 107–26) and compares its features with other contemporary *artes praedicandi* (pp. 99–106), both in Latin; Johnston 1996, passim

Overviews of Lull's system can be found in many places; very accessible is the account of his life, works, and system given by the Centre de Documentació Ramon Llull, Universitat de Barcelona, on the web: http://quisestlullus.narpan.net/eng/1_intro_eng.html (in English).

Citations from Lull 1961 by page.

PART II

Scholastic Sermon Structure

Several *artes praedicandi* recognize the existence and use of different types of sermon structure, whether they are distinguished by their purpose (Chobham: instructing the ignorant, stirring up the lazy, correcting sinners, etc., 18–24), by their following formal artifices (Ars copiosa), or by their use of very specific features, such as kinds of concordance (Wales).[24] In fact, some say that there are as many different kinds as there are competent preachers (Basevorn.243; Waleys.329). More commonly, several treatises recognize that different ways of preaching were used at different times in history. As already mentioned in the introduction, they speak of a *sermo modernus*, the (scholastic) "sermon," that differs formally from the *sermo antiquus*, the "homily." Hesse even goes further and distinguishes: the *sermo antiquissimus* or *postillatio*, used by Christ and the Church Fathers (literal or moral interpretation of Scripture); the *sermo antiquus*, used after the Fathers and before the *modernus* (with thema, protheme, distinction, and subdistinction); the *sermo modernus* (with thema, protheme, division, and subdivision as essential parts); and the *sermo subalternus* (a mixture of *antiquus* and *modernus*). Waleys offers a somewhat different classification, but again with reference to history:

> At some time, after assuming a thema, it [the sermon] was developed without any division, as in many sermons by Augustine and other doctors. At another time, immediately after stating the thema, it was divided without any introduction, as in ancient sermons that were written down and have been preserved until our days. But in our modern time, it is common practice in sermons directed to the clergy to place an introduction to the thema between its statement and its division (356).[25]

Piscario offers a similar distinction adding that the holy doctors of old "preached without taking a thema and ordering the matter of their sermon because they needed no such guidance since they were preaching

---

24 See the respective sections on these treatises.

25 Ps.-Aquinas gives a similar though somewhat confused schema. Basically its *modus antiquus* is an explanation of the gospel followed by a "division and subdivision of the thema"; its second kind is preaching with a distinction; and its third, the scholastic sermon. In the latter, the thema is first announced in Latin and then given in the vernacular (*in vulgari*, 10ra). Notice in this connection that Ps.-Aquinas advises that when preaching in the vernacular, the preacher need not observe the strict order or form of his Latin text (9rb).

under the inspiration of the Holy Spirit," whereas the moderns, "who are not saints nor are thus enlightened by divine grace," have to organize their sermon before they begin (185). The same historical consciousness makes Antoninus say that "no definite mode can be found that has been handed on by the saints and must be followed of necessity" (Antoninus.V).[26] Basevorn even devotes seven of its fifty chapters to a brief historical survey of preaching techniques from God (in the Old Testament) through Christ and St Paul to St Bernard (Basevorn, chapters 6–12).

Tracing the development of the scholastic sermon structure has occupied a number of scholars,[27] and the *artes praedicandi* – formal treatises that describe or teach this structure – form an integral part of this history. Though they differ in completeness, emphasis, and even some details, they offer a fairly consistent type or *Gestalt*, which will be described in the following section.

Before that, a word about my use of the label "scholastic sermon," which I have employed here as well as in earlier publications. The sermon form analysed in this book has been called by several different names, all for good reasons. Medieval writers themselves called it *sermo modernus*. Modern scholars have referred to it as "thematic sermon" because it is typically based upon a thema from which the discourse develops. Other modern scholars speak of it as "university sermon" because its fully developed form originated in the university milieu, predominantly of Paris. Yet "thematic" and "modern" suggest features that can easily create erroneous impressions. While this particular sermon structure indeed originated at the university, a very large portion of the extant sermons built in this form are not specifically connected with the university milieu; and while they are indeed based on a thema, they are primarily not concerned with a "theme" or subject as some modern writers seem to think. The best term for them would indeed be "modern," but I have refrained from using it for the simple reason that the word would have to be placed in quotation marks, again and again. Admittedly, "scholastic sermon" could evoke connections that do, in general, not exist, such as the discussion of major topics of concern

26 For other substantive remarks on *sermo modernus* see also Higden.22, 25, 31, 34, 41, 69, 71; and Alprão.272, 311.

27 A fairly recent presentation is Morenzoni 1995. Much first-hand material can be found in Bériou 1998. See also Jennings 2006.

to theologians like Thomas Aquinas or Bonaventure and the formal method employed in scholastic disputations and *summae*.[28] However, the term "scholastic" would fit well if one considers as genuinely scholastic the urge to divide concepts and issues into parts and order the latter in a numbered sequence. In addition, this particular sermon structure was clearly a by-product of that distinct phase in the development of medieval thought and theology that we call scholasticism.

45 The Scholastic Sermon and Its Parts

In addition to some substantive differences, individual *artes* show minor but noteworthy differences in the style of their presentation. Many are in essence prescriptive, in that they do not merely describe the features of sermon structure (Basevorn)[29] or define them, with the parts of such a definition being explained at greater length (Ars copiosa.19 or Omnis.274–5, on *divisio*), but call attention (*notandum est, sciendum est*) and give rules. For the latter they may use third-person subjunctives in the passive voice: "let the division be taken ..." (Ps.-Bonaventure.8b) or else such modal verbs as *debet, oportet*, or *fiat*: "The protheme should be placed first" (Wales.18v) or "the preacher must choose a thema" (Fusignano.14). Some treatises even address their reader and use the imperative, such as *attende, frater* or *attende, scolaris*, and may even do so from the beginning (*Carissime frater*, in Borgsleben.69). One can of course also find mixtures of such formal differences.

It is probably more useful to distinguish between a static and a progressive exposition. The static mode expounds what a sermon with its parts is or should be like, whereas the progressive mode tells the student reader how to get from A to B to C and so forth: "Take up the thema ... Divide it ... Then you shall argue ..." and so on (Si vis; also Predicacio). Treatises that use the latter mode are likely to present a complete exposition of the scholastic sermon form in the order in which it unfolds from the initially announced thema through division

28 See also the discussion in Wenzel 2005a, pp. 330–2 and 314, 382.

29 The references to individual *artes* in this section indicate examples and are not intended to be exhaustive.

and development to the closing formula. This progression or *Gestalt* can be outlined as follows:

(a) The **thema** is announced.
(b) It is or may be followed by a **protheme** as a kind of prologue, which leads to
(c) A **prayer** for divine assistance.
(d) Then the thema is **repeated** or resumed.
(e) Some kind of connection to the next part is established, which may be what I will call a **bridge passage,** or else a longer
(f) **Introduction of the thema.**
(g) The **division** follows.
(h) The members of the division are **confirmed**. The members are then explained or further **developed** with various processes including
(i) **Subdivisions** and distinctions as well as
(j) Other **processes of dilatation.**
(k) At the end of the development the members may be **tied together**.
(l) Finally, the sermon ends with a **closing formula**, essentially a prayer.

This outline is a conglomerate taken from several *artes*. Its parts and their sequence may be seen best in Wales, Predicacio, Schale; a shorter outline of this kind also appears in Tuderto.37–8.

A different way of presenting the progressive construction of a sermon occurs in Vade, which uses the image of a house that is being built up from its foundation to the roof and internal embellishments. Other *artes* use the image of a tree with its several parts, although more incidentally (Fusignano, Ps.-Aquinas). Such a structure is the medieval preacher's answer to the demand for *dispositio* in classical rhetoric: "Even if [the preacher] has found valid reasons, they are of no use unless he knows how to arrange them (*collocare*), just as in an army, even if one has strong soldiers, they are of no use unless the battle formation is well arranged *(bene disposite)*" (Chobham.268). This structure makes the sermon *artificiosus*, a work constructed with art or a certain technique, in contrast to other ways of preaching. The desire to create it demands that its parts cohere closely, not only logically, by way of the ideas that are developed, but also on the verbal level, by repeating key words and their sounds (see *concordantia* in section 45-h). Hence, one *ars* can claim that a *collatio*, the shorter sermon form, may also be called *colligacio*, because "its members are tied together" (*ad inuicem colligata,* Exercitacio.86ra–va). With such a closely knit structure in his mind the preacher will easily remember his sermon while he is delivering it.

Before turning to these individual parts it may be worth clarifying one or two terms that appear throughout these treatises as part of their specific technical language. A number of works use the four (Aristotelian) causes, in fact begin their presentation with them (see the sections on Wales, Basevorn, Fusignano, Higden, Dic, Eiximenes, Cordoba, Antoninus, and partially in Ps.-Aquinas). They are the efficient cause: the maker of the sermon, where one may distinguish between the *causa efficiens principalis,* God, and the *causa instrumentalis,* the individual preacher. The second is the material cause: the matter of the sermon based on Scripture (Wales). The third is the formal cause: the well-ordered shape of the sermon. And last is the final cause: the purpose and end for which preaching is done, namely God's honour and the salvation of souls. That several of these treatises begin their treatment with these four causes may reflect or parallel the use of the "Aristotelian prologue" that "became popular among lecturers in the arts faculty at the University of Paris" between 1235 and 1245.[30]

Another technical term is *auctoritas,* which I have consistently translated as "authority" but without quotation marks. It is ubiquitous and refers to a text, primarily from Holy Scripture (though authoritative sayings of the Fathers, doctors, even non-Christian philosophers may be included) that is quoted in order to prove a point – in other words, a proof text. Occasionally, it refers to the very thema of the sermon (Alan, Ashby, Auvergne).

There are other terms of whose precise meaning in the *artes praedicandi* modern readers need to be aware. One is *exemplum,* which will be discussed in section 49. Another is *figura,* referring to a biblical person or event that may have a spiritual or moral meaning; the term could be translated as "type" or "symbol" but not "figure of speech."'[31] Still others are *clavis* and *sufficientia* (see 45-g), *facies* (45-j), *pes sermonis* (45-e), and *manuductio* (45-f), whose technical meanings will be clarified in their respective sections.

The parts of the scholastic sermon will be discussed sequentially in the following sections, 45-a to 45-l, with citations of the respective

30 Cf. Minnis and Scott 1988, pp. 198–200.
31 Cf. Jennings 2003, p. 68.

treatise in abbreviated form, often followed by a reference to a page or folio (see the Abbreviations above, pp. xi–xii). It must be emphasized that some of these features or steps in the scholastic sermon are in fact logical processes that may occur in several different places. For example, dividing a sentence or a concept into its parts, while forming a distinct step in the structuring of the sermon (45-g), is also a procedure that may be applied in the protheme (45-b) or in the development of the sermon (45-i). Similarly, confirmation of the parts of a division (45-h) occurs not only after the division (45-g) but wherever any authority is divided. Another case in point is the requirement to find a *sufficientia*: many *artes* treat this as an aspect of division (45-g), but some consider it also when they deal with the bridge passage (45-e).

45-a Thema

The defining element of the sermon form which is described, illustrated, and taught by the *artes praedicandi* is the thema: a word or string of words taken from Scripture upon which the entire sermon is built. It is mentioned in every treatise that deals with the structure of the scholastic sermon, although three early treatises do not use the term itself: Alan, Ashby, and Auvergne. Yet Alan clearly teaches to begin a sermon with what he calls an *auctoritas*, that is, a biblical or patristic quotation used as the sermon's foundation. Ashby similarly says, "Let an *auctoritas* be announced, which shall be the subject matter of the entire sermon" (*sermonis tocius materia*) (Ashby.28), and the same usage of *auctoritas* and *materia* occurs in Auvergne (199).[32]

In fact, the thema is defined as *materia* by a number of treatises: "*Thema* is called in Greek what we call *materia* in Latin" (Waleys.341; Wales.18v).[33] Hence, the thema is "as it were the foundation of the whole

32 The very long *Rudimentum doctrinae* by Guibert of Tournai, which does not deal with sermon structure explicitly (see above, section 10), apparently does not use "thema" either but instead speaks of *materia*.

33 But notice that Omnis distinguishes between the two terms: "After the thema has been announced, the *materia* of the sermon must right away be stated in a general and undifferentiated (*permiste*) way, and at once be applied to the announced thema" (262). Ps.-Aquinas declares that "thema" means the beginning (*principium*) of the sermon, or its protheme (*prelocutio*), or "whatever is said in the thema and its division" (3va–b).

work ... in which everything that is to be said is virtually contained" (Wales.18v and Predicacio; Alprão.265; cf. Exercitacio). The word itself seems to have been frequent in school and rhetorical texts from late antiquity on[34] and recurs also in the poetic arts of Geoffrey of Vinsauf,[35] Eberhard of Bethun,[36] and John of Garland.[37] Chobham is clearly aware of the use of *thema* among poets and rhetoricians (260–1).

The thema of a sermon is sometimes likened to the root of a tree (Cordoba.332; Nota.165v – but notice the different use of *radix* below in sections 45-e and 45-g; Exercitacio) or the foundation of a house (Vade. passim; Chobham.27; Wales.18v etc.; Piscario.180; Fusignano.16; Exercitacio). Cordoba offers a string of images: "The thema is related to the sermon as a vessel [*vas*] to an edifice, the root to a tree, the spring to its rivulets, the sun to its rays, and the head to the body" (332).

Those *artes* that deal explicitly with the thema often discuss it at some length and even specify a number of rules:[38]

(1) It must be taken from Scripture (Wales, Basevorn.250–3, Piscario, Fusignano, Dic, Ars copiosa, Waleys, Higden, Tuderto, Hesse, Schale, Omnis, Eiximenes, Alprão, Cordoba, Vade, Circa, Nota, Ps.-Aquinas, Exercitacio). Chobham declares: "No thema must be given except a theological one. Authorities from moral philosophers or poets are to be taken for embellishment or for support of the divine word, but not to lay down the foundation"

34 Quintilian: "Scholarum consuetudo, in quibus certa quaedam ponuntur quae themata dicimus" (*Institutiones* 4.2.28; cf. 4.2.90; in Quintilian, *Institutio oratoria*, ed. H.E. Butler and Donald A. Russell, 4 vols, Loeb Classical Library 124–7, 494 (Cambridge, MA, 1920, 2001), 2:64 and 100); Jerome, prologue to the Book of Esther: "Sicut solitum est scolaribus disciplinis sumpto themate excogitare quibus verbis uti poterit qui iniuriam passus est vel ille qui iniuriam fecit," in *Biblia sacra iuxta Vulgatam versionem*, ed. R. Weber et al., 2 vols (Stuttgart, 1983), 1:712. See also Bonner 1949, p. 51; Lausberg 1960, vol. 2, p. 952, under thème.

35 Geoffrey of Vinsauf, *Poetria nova*, line 112 and passim; in Faral 1958, p. 200, etc.

36 Eberhard of Bethun, *Laborintus*, line 269 and passim; in Faral 1958, p. 346, etc.

37 John of Garland, *Parisiana poetria* 1.166, and especially 4.100; in Lawler 1974, pp. 12 and 62.

38 Best perhaps in Basevorn.249–60 and Higden.15–25, more briefly in Hesse.349. Others: Wales.18v, 19v–20; Piscario.180; Fusignano.14–26; Dic.65–6; Ars copiosa.17–18; Ad erudicionem.37r–v; Waleys.341–9; Schale.107; Omnis.261; Eiximenes.332–3; Alprão.265–9; Cordoba.332–4; Vade.168–72; In accepcione.30vb; Nota.165v; Ps.-Aquinas.3va.

(Chobham.274). Though the gospels, the Pauline epistles, the Psalms, and "the books of Salomon" are occasionally given preference (Alan.113, "maxime," but this is called an "error" in Basevorn.264), any book of the Bible may serve as source, and some *artes* even discuss individual books (Basevorn.264–6, adding lists of themata appropriate to sermons *de tempore, de sanctis,* for special occasions, and *ad status,* 266–8). Ars copiosa has an entire "preamble" listing the canonical books of the Bible, as does Antoninus. If the thema is taken from the Old Testament, it should be interpreted or explained with the gospels (Ars copiosa). In general, the *artes* speak against using a quasi-biblical text from the liturgy (e.g., Waleys.342; Higden.17–18), but Exercitacio allows using a biblical text with a change of a word as well as a non-biblical text as these occur in the liturgy (thereby distinguishing *modus proprius, largus, and largissimus,* 86va). Further, its text should be taken from the standard (Latin) translation (Basevorn.251; Higden). Some *artes* further consider such matters as the omission of function words, using words with different denotations, cropping of clauses, etc., and allow function words and interjections that are found in the biblical text to be omitted (e.g., Basevorn.251–2; Waleys.344–5; Higden.18–19). Cordoba further allows proverbs in Latin or in the vernacular to be occasionally used as the thema, "for the sake of novelty" (333).

(2) It must be short (Ars copiosa, Cordoba, Circa, In accepcione), especially in sermons to the clergy (Waleys), but not too short (Hesse, Ps.-Aquinas).

(3) It must be a complete, independent, grammatically correct sentence (Ars copiosa: *vocis congruitas*), making full sense (Wales, Basevorn.250, Fusignano, Dic, Ars copiosa, Hesse, Schale, Alprão, Cordoba, Higden, Omnis, Borgsleben, Vade, Ps.-Aquinas, Exercitacio). Conjunctions and adverbs (Fusignano) must, and other parts (Waleys, Higden) found in the biblical text may, be omitted; other changes, too, are permissible (Ars copiosa, Waleys, Higden). An example of an incomplete thema that is to be avoided is *Ascendente Iesu in navicula* ("As Jesus entered a small boat," Matthew 8:23: Ars copiosa, Quamvis, Vade).

(4) It must be clear (Higden, Schale, Borgsleben) and agree with its biblical context (Fusignano; Waleys.347–9; Hesse: *bene quotatum*).

(5) It must be appropriate for the occasion, that is, for the respective Sunday, or feast day, or the saint whose feast is being celebrated

(Wales, Basevorn.249–50, 264–6; Fusignano, Quamvis, Waleys, Ars copiosa, Higden, Hesse, Schale, Omnis, Eiximenes, Cordoba, Exercitacio). Generally, on Sundays and feast days the thema should be taken from either the gospel or epistle lection; some *artes* allow the use of material from a Mass text (gradual, etc., for example Fusignano, Exercitacio), while others speak against it (see above). On saints' feasts, the thema may be taken from the gospel or epistle lection, or from anywhere in the Bible, as long as it fits the saint or feast celebrated.[39] Thus, *Ave Maria* will serve well for the feast of the Annunciation but not for the Assumption of Mary (Ars copiosa.18), and St Stephen should be celebrated with a sermon that contains the word "stone" (Cordoba.334). Waleys and Eiximenes note the "innovation" of choosing a thema from the preceding Sunday for the feast of a saint that occurs during the week.[40]

Eiximenes reports the same practice in sermons for the dead (332–3). Ars copiosa begins its discussion of this point with the general statement that the thema must fit the subject matter of the sermon (17v) and then gives specific recommendations for Sundays and feast days. For sermons for the dead it suggests finding a thema that somehow expresses the name of the dead person or anything connected with his or her life (17v, without examples). Some authors give a few examples (e.g., Higden.16–17), while others furnish extensive lists of fitting themata for different occasions (best seen in Basevorn.266–8, though Charland omits most of the text; see also Wales.23–6).

(6) Its terms should be words that occur frequently in Scripture, so that in the following division the preacher can readily find verbal material for the needed concordances (Basevorn.257–8, Waleys.345–6, explaining *concordancia vocalis* and *realis*; Quamvis; Higden; Hesse; Schale; Borgsleben; In accepcione), which must be *copiosus* (Ars copiosa.17v), *fecundus* (Omnis), or *fructuosus* (Alprão.267). Also, these terms should not be "bad" or vulgar words (or sound vulgar in the vernacular), and if they are unusual

39 Not all preachers, including authors of *artes predicandi*, obeyed this rule. St Antoninus of Florence, for example, has no difficulty in applying the description of the rich man (Luke 16.19) to St Gregory (Antoninus.V.2).

40 See Wenzel 2005a, p. 64 and n. 26. The same idea occurs in Eiximenes.332.

or foreign (*peregrina*), the preacher must explain them (Ars copiosa.17v).

(7) It must have three words or their equivalents (Basevorn.254–7: no more than three) or yield at least three (or more) members for the division (Ars copiosa.17, Higden, Omnis). Hesse says that four terms suffice, and at least two are necessary, not counting indefinite pronouns (*consignificativa*) like *omnis*, *quidam*, etc.

To these general rules, some *artes* add more specific ones:

(8) The preacher should carefully examine the words of his thema. Several *artes* require that he specifically consider the grammatical person used in the thema and to whom it is directed (Ps.-Bonaventure, Rochelle, Ars copiosa), or other aspects of its verbs, such as person, tense, mood (Rochelle). Such analysis will show that the thema expresses various modes, such as prayer, threat, exhortation, etc. (Ars copiosa.17; cf. Ps.-Bonaventure; Rochelle.202–4; Higden.46; Dic; Tuderto; Exercitacio), and these indicate the biblical author's main intention, which the preacher should point out in his sermon, specifically in the bridge passage (Hic; see section 45-e). Auvergne extends the required examination to other words in the thema and their grammatical aspects (207–9). More broadly, Tuderto gives six rules for considering the words of the thema, namely what they mean, whether they can be expounded according to the four scriptural senses, or according to the four (Aristotelian) causes, their good or bad effect, and whether they denote something noble or, conversely, blameworthy (8–16). Eiximenes similarly specifies such analysis, for purposes of the development (322–3); its author, incidentally, speaks of the four causes at various places (304–6, 321, 324, 330).

(9) In choosing his thema, the preacher should try to say something edifying (Dic.65–6), and he must not offend his audience (Dic).

(10) Higden adds that the thema should be such as to allow the protheme to be taken from it (25).

Some *artes* add further that the preacher should identify the source of the thema. Waleys, for instance, says that the book and chapter of Scripture from where the thema is taken must be given, though Psalm numbers are usually omitted. This should certainly be observed when one writes out the sermon, though in oral delivery practices vary

(Waleys.346–7). Shorter rules on this matter appear in Chobham.286, Basevorn.268, Higden.34, Eiximenes.333, and Hic (148, *cum sua cotacione*).

45-b Protheme

A number of *artes* teach that after the thema has been announced, it may be followed by a protheme, also called *antethema* or other terms.[41] Its function is manifold. Chobham, following its general orientation to classical rhetoric, considers it the first part of a speech and calls it *exordium, proemium, prologus, prefatio, principium, protosermo, insinuatio,* or *prothema*. It prepares the audience for what is to follow and makes them benevolent, attentive, and docile.[42] To "capture the audience's benevolence" the preacher may speak about himself, showing his humility and desire to lead his audience to salvation (263–5 and 269–72; cf. Alan.113). Later treatises echo this[43] but focus more on the protheme's function of leading to prayer (see the following section):

> After the thema has been announced and identified, one must proceed to the *antethema* (or *prothema*, which is the same), which brings an imploration of divine help, grace, or favour, or of anything else that refers

---

41 The protheme is discussed in: Ashby.26–7 (*prohemium, prologus*); Chobham.262–5; Rochelle.196 (briefly); Wales.18v, 19v–20; Predicacio.341; Basevorn.259–60, 284 ff.; Piscario.198 (referring to his practice); Fusignano.26; Waleys.350; Higden.25–30; perhaps Tuderto.37–40 (speaking of *thematis introductio* and *verbum preambulum*); Hesse.348–56; Schale.107; Eiximenes.332–3; Cordoba.332–3; Borgsleben.71–4; In accepcione.30vb; Ps.-Aquinas.passim (*prelocutio*); Exercitacio.87ra–b (*prohemium*). The term *antethema* is used, either by itself or as an alternative to *prothema*, by Wales, Predicacio, In accepcione, Basevorn, Waleys, Higden, and Schale. Chobham seems to have been the first historically to call this part *prothema*.

42 This triad is based on Cicero, *De inventione* 1.15.20, in Cicero, *De inventione, De optimo genere oratorum, Topica*, ed. H.M. Hubbell, Loeb Classical Library 386 (Cambridge, MA, 1976), pp. 40–2; *Ad Herennium* 1.4.7, in Ps.-Cicero, *Ad C. Herennium de ratione dicendi*, ed. Harry Caplan, Loeb Classical Library 403 (Cambridge, MA, 1961), p. 12; and Augustine, *De doctrina christiana* 4.2.3, in Augustine, *De doctrina Christiana*, ed. and trans. R.P.H. Green (Oxford, 1995), p. 196. It appears in Alan, Ashby, Chobham, Higden, Cordoba.

43 Basevorn devotes chapter XXIV to rendering the audience benevolent, which he calls *auditus allectio*, in what would correspond to the protheme, for which he suggests a number of methods, such as telling something that catches the audience's interest or curiosity, or that might frighten them, and so on (Basevorn.260–2; taken over in shortened form by Higden.32–4).

> to the preacher, to preaching, or to the audience, so that they may fittingly hear or practise it. (Schale.107; cf. Higden.25–6)

Or more briefly: "The protheme must be said in the beginning so that divine grace and wisdom may be asked for. And it is called *prothema* as if to say 'before the thema,' just as we call *prologus* what comes before the things that are to be said in what follows" (Wales.18v). Hence its substance should agree with the general subject of the sermon (Chobham.265). Rochelle states succinctly that the protheme should declare the preacher's insufficiency, excite the audience's devotion to pray, and praise God's goodness in bestowing his grace on the preacher to teach and the people to hear (204).

But in discussing what they call *prothema* in more detail, the *artes* do not show the same uniformity and precision as they do with the thema, and the student of preaching arts will have to be aware of significant peculiarities in individual works as well as of changes over time. In addition, some treatises call the protheme *introductio*, which may cause some confusion because another major feature of the scholastic sermon is the *introductio thematis* (see below in 45-f; Lull.399 speaks of *introitus sermonis*, which may be the protheme). Eiximenes does so but distinguishes between the two clearly and considers them two of the three constituent parts of the "modern" sermon. Alprão similarly speaks of *introductio* as one of the three constituent parts of the sermon but seems to refer by it to the introduction of the thema (264; the treatise in its extant form may be incomplete, missing the announced second part).

The richest treatise in this respect is Hesse. In its discussion of four different (historical) modes it includes *prothema* as an essential part in the *modus modernus, antiquus,* and *subalternus* (see above, p. 26). (a) In the *modus modernus*, the *prothema* comes before the division and is defined as "a prelocution made for the confirmation of the terms posited in the thema that are to be preached about" (prelocutio facta pro approbatione terminorum predicabilium in themate positorum, 340). It must be made from quotations from Scripture, or from philosophers, or from examples taken from nature; it should not have a division; it must concord with the thema; it must end with a quotation of the thema; and it is followed by the division. (b) For the *modus antiquus*, Hesse states as a general rule: "Whatever is said between the thema and its division or distinction is the protheme" (Quicquid dicitur inter thema et eius divisionem vel distinctionem, prothema est, 353). (c) The *modus subalternus* mentions *prothema* but does not discuss it further. It would therefore seem that Hesse's *prothema* resembles what in most other *artes* is considered the introduction of the thema. It should also be noted that the presence of a protheme distinguishes the sermon from a collation (below, section 48).

Another term used for the protheme is *preambulum* (Tuderto, Eiximenes, Alprão, Borgsleben). Tuderto introduces it almost as an afterthought. In chapter V, on *ordinatio,* it lists eight parts of a sermon (see above, p. 24), which do not include a protheme. But then (there seems to be some confusion in the text as edited) it says that "before the thema is announced we should place some preamble *(quoddam verbum preambulum*[44] *praemittere),* either in the form of an excuse or as an introduction *(ingressus)* to what needs to be explained by the thema that is to be announced" (40). The author illustrates this part with two examples from *collationes* he says he had made at funerals.

It is therefore evident that the practice of beginning with a protheme as well as its form could differ and that it changed in the course of two or three centuries. In earlier *artes* the protheme is said to be, or to begin with, a biblical quotation of its own which differs from the thema but should have some verbal or notional agreement (Rochelle.196, 204; cf. Wales.19v; Ps.-Aquinas.3va–4rb). This seems to have been standard practice in the thirteenth century.[45] But in the next century Basevorn considered this older practice less useful (Basevorn.259–60), and following him Higden attributed it to *antiqui,* declaring that *moderni* "more fittingly" (*decencius*) extract the protheme from the thema itself (Higden.25). This change in the conception and practice of the protheme is neatly reflected in Cordoba, which declares:

> According to the ancient technique, after the thema a protheme was set up, which was to agree with the thema ... But in our modern technique this has been abolished, and the intention [of the preacher] is better founded on the words of the main thema, by beginning at once, after the main thema has been applied to the Virgin, with "She is ..." But I think that the protheme is a kind of exordium, which should contain three things

44 Babcock's edition reads *perambulum.*

45 Good collections of material from *prothemata* in thirteenth-century university sermons are given in Kaeppeli 1946 and Schneyer 1968. Notice that Ars copiosa is much concerned with demanding that, if the protheme and thema are the same text or share an important word, their respective divisions should be different (16v).

> that make the audience attentive, docile, and benevolent. Therefore, after announcing his thema, the preacher should set forth the usefulness, the order of his speech, and his audience's devotion ... Or else, in place of the protheme he may present some things that make his audience attentive to the word of God, or he may begin with comparing his sermon to food for the body ... (332–3)

In any case, the protheme should be somehow related to the announced thema. *Artes* that are specific about this relationship require vocal or notional concordance (Rochelle, Wales, Fusignano, Ars copiosa, Hesse), and Higden considers in some detail how the protheme is to be extracted from themata that have only one term (for instance, *Intellige*) or more than one (26–8). In order to achieve such concordance the preacher must select his thema carefully, as was noted in the preceding section 45-a (see especially Basevorn.259).

If the preacher wants to speak of the entire gospel lection, he should, in his protheme, quote the beginning of the lection (Fusignano.26). This biblical quotation may then be subjected to the same processes of division and development as the main thema (Basevorn.259–60). In this regard, Ars copiosa distinguishes between sermons *ad populum* and those *ad clerum*. In the former it is not necessary to base the protheme on a biblical text: it may be taken from the Bible or from *doctores* of the Church. In *sermones ad clerum*, however, the protheme must be either the same as the thema, or another biblical text which agrees with the thema in either verbal form or meaning (16r–v). More generally, at the end of his longer discussion of extracting the protheme from the thema, Higden reports that some preachers do not extract the protheme from the thema or another biblical text but instead begin with a popular proverb, or in fact omit it altogether and go from the announced thema directly to the prayer (29–30). Finally, Schale says that it is not mandatory (*non requiritur*) that the protheme agree with the thema vocally or notionally, but if it does, so much the better (107).

As to this agreement, Ars copiosa requires that the protheme should somehow reflect the "first and principal" term of the thema if possible; if not, it should reflect its last one (cf. Fusignano.26). Ars copiosa further insists that equivocation, such as concording *mane*, "stay," with *mane*, "morning," must be avoided (16v). If the protheme speaks of qualities of the preacher, these must be confirmed with biblical or other proof. Its last point should always speak of grace, so as to lead naturally to the prayer. And if it is divided and developed, this should be done differently from the division and development of the thema. Borgsleben devotes its final section to making *introducciones* or a *praeambulum* in sermons *ad populum*, specifying three ways: by something opposite to the words of the thema, by some subject matter that touches upon the thema in its good or bad meaning, or by giving a division, distinction, or noteworthy quotation; these possibilities are then discussed and illustrated at some length. As a general rule the protheme should be relatively short (Wales, Fusignano, Hesse, Ars copiosa), and Eiximenes specifies that it should not take more time than saying an Our Father (333).

45-c Initial Prayer

"It is customary that after announcing and identifying the thema the preacher, before he begins his sermon, exhorts the people to pray to God for grace for himself and for his audience, namely that he may preach the word of God worthily and that the people may hear it to their benefit" (Waleys.349).[46] The reason for this is that "it is generally the custom in the Church that in every act everyone should strengthen himself by prayer" (Chobham.261), for which occasionally the authority of Plato is invoked.[47]

Basevorn, as he does so often, notes varying practices among various preachers. For instance, some preachers place such a prayer for grace or peace even before they announce the thema, which he considers *vitiosum*. Rather – as already indicated in the preceding section – the prayer, *oratio*,[48] should follow the announcement of the thema. It may do so at once, with only a few introductory words and the exhortation *Rogemus Dominum* (Fusignano.26), or it may come at the end of a somewhat longer section, the protheme. In the latter case, Basevorn says that it should be verbally linked to what has preceded. As to the prayer itself, several artes, especially later ones, specify the *Ave Maria* (Wales, Tuderto, Eiximenes, Cordoba, Ps.-Aquinas; see also Fusignano, Waleys),

46 The introductory prayer is discussed in Chobham.261–2; Basevorn.262–4; Fusignano.14, 26–8; Waleys.349–50; Higden.26 and 30–2; Tuderto.38; Schale.107; Eiximenes.333; Cordoba.332–3; In accepcione.30vb; Ps.-Aquinas.9vb. Some *artes* do not discuss it explicitly but use it in an example: Predicacio.342; also Wales.19; Ars copiosa.16vb.

47 In Chobham.261, Basevorn.262, Waleys.331, Higden.30; Plato's advice (cf. *Timaeus* C27) is quoted in Boethius, *Consolation*, 3.pr. 9.32, in Boethius, *Philosophiae consolatio*, ed. Ludwig Bieler, CCSL 94 (Turnhout, 1957), p. 51, and Boethius is likewise quoted in this connection in Basevorn.262 and Higden.30.

48 Notice that the word *oratio* can also mean "sentence" or "speech."

and Higden allows it (*si placuerit*) together with the prayer for divine help. Eiximenes.333 says that in some countries the *Ave Maria* is prayed silently (so also Tuderto.38), in others recited aloud. Cordoba adds that on Good Friday the Salutation of Mary is not used; instead one should "say the Our Father or the prayer to the Cross" (331). Similarly Fusignano observes that "in sermons for the dead ... such a prayer is usually not said, perhaps because formerly in sermons of this kind the preacher was more concerned with praising the deceased and consoling his friends than with explaining Sacred Scripture" (28). Some *artes* do not deal with the prayer explicitly but mention it in connection with the protheme or present just such a formula in their examples of prothemes (Wales.18v–19, Ars copiosa.16v, In accepcione.30vb). This prayer at the opening of the sermon should not be confused with the stipulation to pray at its end, for which see below (section 45-l).

In actual sermons, both Latin and vernacular, the invitation to say an *Ave Maria* or *Pater Noster*, or both, occurs innumerable times. Some sermons add at the same place a longer *recommendatio* or intercessory prayer, usually for patrons, rulers, the living, and the dead.[49] Among the *artes* here studied only Schale includes a remark about this practice, speaking of *preces* (107).

45-d Repetition of the Thema

Those *artes* that deal with the entire structure of the scholastic sermon specify that after the completed protheme and initial prayer the already announced thema of the sermon is to be repeated or "resumed."[50] Basevorn, Waleys, and Higden add that in the repetition the quotation must be identified by book and chapter as it had been at the original citation. Basevorn considers it *vitiosum* to say *ubi prius* ("as above," 269) instead of quoting book and chapter again, but allows that one may do so in the delivery of the sermon, whereas in writing it out one must cite the source explicitly. Notice, however, that extant sermons are replete

49 Most frequently in monastic sermons. For some examples see Wenzel 2005a, pp. 196, 286.

50 Wales.19; Predicacio.341, 342; Basevorn.268–9; Waleys.355; Higden.34; Schale.107; In accepcione.30vb. Probably also Ps.-Aquinas.10ra and Alprão.300 and 309. Tuderto.37 and 44 is not entirely clear.

with *ubi prius*'s. Schale uniquely demands that "after the ante-thema and prayers the thema is to be recited without identification and to be explained in the vernacular" (107).

45-e Bridge Passage

After what may be considered parts of a prologue that end with the resumption of the thema (sections 45-a to 45-d above), the main development of the sermon begins with an introduction of the thema (*introductio thematis*), which will be discussed in the next section. But whether one builds a sermon with all the parts analysed so far, or more simply proceeds from the first announcement of the thema to the introduction, or even more simply goes immediately to the division, a transitional statement is desirable which applies or adapts the chosen thema to the subject matter and intention of the sermon. This I shall call the "bridge passage." Some *artes* declare that such a sentence should "connote" what the thema contains, such as: "These words can be applied to our information" (Piscario.180, 187), and others similarly speak of "applying" (Wales.19) or "adapting" the thema (Fusignano.30: *coaptari*). Some *artes* even have a special name for it. Thus, Fusignano calls it *prelibacio* (32). More specifically, Dic names it *pes* or rather *pedis posicio* and says that "it shows the main intent of the introduction" (Pedis posicio ostendit introduccionis principalem intentum).[51] This curious use of *pes* also appears in other minor *artes*.[52] Hic speaks of *pes vel fundamentum*, whereas Vade similarly defines *pedis posicio* as "the foundation (*fundamentum*) which is abstracted from the thema, agrees with the end [i.e., purpose of the sermon], and underlies the division." Vade thus uses the term *fundamentum* in two different senses, referring to the bridge passage as well as the thema itself. Still another term for this introductory sentence is *radix* (Rochelle.passim, also in Ars copiosa.17 and passim). Ars copiosa, for instance, first says that the thema should be adapted or introduced (*adaptari siue ... manuduci*, 18) to the following division, and then adds an entire section on what it now calls the *radix sermonis*, giving a number of rules for it (18–19). The term *radix* is of

51 Dic.66–9 (especially at 2.b–c) and 73, similarly Circa.102r–v (for *intentum* the reading *intellectum* is possible).

52 Circa.102r–v; Hic.150; Nota.165v–6; and Vade.176.

course equivocal because elsewhere it is used for the thema itself (Cordoba.332; Nota.165v). It may well be that the peculiar term *pes* or *pedis posicio* was introduced in order to avoid such confusion.

In the attempt to apply the thema to the intention and matter of his sermon and thereby establish a logical relationship between thema, introduction, and the following division, the preacher is advised to examine his chosen thema carefully and determine who the speaker is and what his intention is (Ps.-Bonaventure, though without speaking of a bridge passage; Rochelle; Ars copiosa; Hic; Exercitacio; see section 45-a). This process is described most analytically in Rochelle, which considers in detail the grammatical person/persons that is/are contained in the thema and, in case it is directed to a second person, what its mode is: question, threat, derision, exhortation, petition, and so forth (Rochelle.202; recurring in Ars copiosa.17, both using *radix*). Later *artes* then equally consider the grammatical person in the thema and, more important, the intentions that can be found in biblical quotations (teaching a truth, raising a question or doubt, condemning vices, etc.). This intention may then be expressed in the bridge passage (Circa.102v). A very brief example is the thema *Jesus, son of David, have pity on me,* which is followed by the bridge passage. "This is the voice of one asking for help" (Rochelle.204; Ars copiosa.17). A longer example is "Matthew 20: *Why do you stand here idle all day*? Here Our Lord reproaches people who are idle and fail to work in this life" (Ps.-Bonaventure.8b). Some *artes* do not explicitly discuss this process but nonetheless apply it in some of their illustrative examples (for instance, Basevorn.256 or Higden.46–7). The bridge passage, therefore, is essentially a brief introduction to the following division.

Ars copiosa recognizes the desirability of such a passage also before subdivisions and elsewhere; in a longer passage it calls this device or procedure *artificium* (25v–7). Ad erudicionem similarly says more shortly: "the members of a distinction must be based on an *artificium* that should go before ..." (38).

45-f Introduction of the Thema

"And then [i.e., after the repetition of the thema] another brief and fitting introduction should be made which shows that the thema was chosen for good reason" (Et tunc fiat alia breuis decensque introduccio vt videatur quod thema fuit racionabiliter sumptum, Predicacio.341). Nearly all *artes* speak of such an *introductio thematis*.[53] Its function is to lead from the announced thema to the division, to express or declare "something to which the division of the thema can be adapted" or applied (aliquid cui thematis diuisio coaptari possit, Fusignano.30), to establish "a fitting application of the thema" (competens applicatio thematis, Wales.19; cf. Omnis.262; and Hesse.349: *pro approbatione* of the terms in the thema), or "in which the meaning of the entire thema is contained and enclosed" (in quo contineatur et claudatur sentencia tocius thematis, Hic.150). Tuderto judges this part "very necessary" (41), while Eiximenes.332 and Alprão.264 consider it one of the three main parts of the sermon. In other words, the *introductio thematic* introduces not only the thema but also its following division (Basevorn.284).

This *introductio thematis* may be made in different forms, namely, with the help of a popular proverb; a simile from nature, human behavior, or history; a scriptural authority, sometimes with its own division; a quotation from a saintly author, philosopher, or poet; any type of argument (syllogism, induction, enthymeme, or example); a distinction made by the preacher himself; or even a moralized fable or story (Cordoba.336). If this introduction is a biblical quotation, it should share one word with the thema or at least agree with it in meaning; a quotation from another author should agree in meaning (Hesse.349–50, with examples). To these standard modes, some *artes* add definition or description (Omnis.266–7); a question (Omnis.269–71; Tuderto.46–51; Eiximenes.333; Alprão.318–19, Cordoba.336) or solution of a doubt (Eiximenes.334–5); stating the opposite (Borgsleben.72; Omnis.271–2); a moralized fable (Cordoba.336; cf. Chobham.266) or allegory (called *pulchra fictio*, Cordoba.336); or the gospel or epistle text (Schale.107v). For the introduction that uses an example from human behaviour, three artes use the term *manuductio*,[54] a very rare word in the preaching arts I have studied (Ars copiosa.18v; Quamvis.110 and passim; and the derived Higden.35, 38). As some *artes* point out, the various possibilities

53 Chobham.266, 272–84; Wales.19, 20r–v; Basevorn.269–73; Fusignano.30, without calling it thus; Waleys.357–69; Higden.35–43; Predicacio.341–2; Dic.66–8; Quamvis.110–14; Ars copiosa.18 without using the term; Tuderto.41–68; Schale.107r–v; Eiximenes.333–5; Alprão.264, 265, 269–72; Cordoba.334–7; Borgsleben.71–4; Omnis.262–74; Hic.150; Vade.172–6; Circa.102; In accepcione.30vb–1ra; Nota.165v–6; Ps.-Aquinas.10ra. Notice that Hesse calls it *prothema* (350–2), see above, section 45-b.

54 Jennings 1991 points out that the word is attested from the ninth century on (p. 35, n. 40) but was not aware of Quamvis.

of *introductio* will work only with themata that contain two or more words or terms. In the case of single-term themata, one can use an authority, divide it into three parts, and then continue (Basevorn.272–3; Higden.41–3). At its end, the introduction should restate the thema (Hesse.358 and others).

The various forms are listed in different arrangements, and they are usually illustrated with examples that may consist of only one or two sentences (Fusignano) or fairly lengthy paragraphs (Tuderto, Omnis, and others). Waleys places these modes in a logical frame by categorizing them in terms of their accidents (length, source) and essential form (narrative or argumentative; 357–9). Such careful attention to the various modes of the introduction is carried to great length in Alprão.269–324, discussing ten main modes, which include division (i.e., of a scriptural quotation used in the introduction) and *figura*, a short narrative from Scripture which is then divided and explained. Similar lists of ten modes occur in other Iberian writers, such as Eiximenes.333–5 and Cordoba.334–7, though their items differ somewhat in name and arrangement. Furthermore, Waleys analyses and illustrates the use of a syllogism and its parts, especially the minor premise, at greater length (362–4, distinguishing the modus *argumentativus* from the *modus narrativus*). It is interesting to note that several times its Dominican author stresses that, in using an argumentative introduction, the preacher should form a syllogism and so on "in his heart" and reflect on it but need not present it explicitly and in proper sequence, since in preaching it is not necessary to prove the truth of the thema but rather point out its usefulness. A similar statement appears more succinctly in Wales ("quasi sillogistice, non observata forma sillogisandi sed virtute ... et hoc cum breuitate," 20). A similarly detailed and even longer analysis of using a syllogism and its parts in the *introductio* appears in Alprão.270–301.

A few treatises do not deal separately with such an *introductio* at all (Ashby, Si vis, Ps.-Aquinas), while others discuss it without naming it thus (Fusignano.32; Ars copiosa.18v–19) or else use the word *introitus* (Wales.20; Eiximenes: *introitus ad thema*, 335) and even *prothema* (Hesse.349–52). Chobham, as usual following classical rhetoric, considers it both under the parts of a speech (266) and under invention (272–84) and gives equivalents to the variety of introductions listed above except for argumentation. Several works are not entirely clear about whether they intend the protheme or the *introductio*, or in fact distinguish between the two (Hic, Borgsleben near the end, Circa,

Nota, Ps.-Aquinas). Treatises that speak of historically different forms of preaching stress that the *introductio thematis* is part of the "modern" sermon (Hesse.349–52, calling it *prothema*; Eiximenes.332). Tuderto emphasizes that it is a necessary part of the sermon (41), while Vade, in following its controlling image, considers it the wall of a house with four sides, that is, introducing the thema with an authority, reason, exemplum, or "induction" (172–6).

The longer discussions reveal that in scholastic preaching the *introductio thematis* became a piece of highly crafted verbal art. Basevorn even points out that to the modes used at Oxford – arranged here as seven – the University of Paris adds an eighth (271). At the same time he says that the *introductio* should be short (269; cf. Wales.20; Predicacio.341; Waleys.357) and may be omitted altogether, while Waleys criticizes preachers who elaborate it at such length that, when they come to the division, they have run out of time (357). To the demand for brevity, Dic adds that the *introductio* must be clear, in order to be understood by the audience (*leuis*, 67).

45-g Division

Nearly all *artes* here considered speak of a *divisio* (*thematis*),[55] which together with the thema and the following development is one of the three (Ps.-Bonaventure.8) or four (Ashby.905; Ps.-Aquinas.3vb; Hesse.348–9) or six (Chobham.262) main parts of the "modern" or scholastic sermon and in fact in Schale is called the sermon's *fundamentum* (107v). In it, the quoted thema is divided into a number of parts (*partes, membra*), which then serve as the starting points for further

55 The division is discussed at Ashby.28; Chobham.266, 284–93; Thetford.84–8; Ps.-Bonaventure.8–16; Auvergne.204 (one form of *distinctio*, but does not really deal with division of the thema); Rochelle (the branches off the trunk, throughout); Wales.19 and passim; Predicacio.340; Ad habendum.313–14 (one way to generate matter); Basevorn.273–5; Piscario.180–2; Fusignano.28–36; Dic.68–9; Quamvis.114–20; Ars copiosa.19–23v; Ad erudicionem.37v–8; Waleys.368–79; Higden.21–3, 43–54; Tuderto.1–17 and passim; Hesse.352; Schale.107v; Omnis.274–8; Eiximenes: 335–9; Alprão.264, 324–6; Antoninus.passim; Alcok.entire treatise; Cordoba.337–41; Borgsleben.69–70; Hic.150–2; Vade.178; Circa.102v–3; In accepcione.31ra–b; Nota.166r–v; Si vis.29; Ps.-Aquinas.10ra; Exercitacio.87rb–8rb; In predicatore.82rb; Lull.398–9. For *divisio* as a method of development (Alan and Auvergne) see further section 45-i.

development. The basic function of the division, thus, is to unfold the meaning of the chosen thema and thereby to provide the preacher with ample material for his discourse: "Modern preachers have invented dividing the thema – what the ancients did not used to do – not simply for elegance, as some believe, but because it is useful to the preacher, because dividing the thema into several members provides the opportunity of dilatation for the further development of the sermon" (Non enim propter solam curiositatem, sicut aliqui credunt, invenerunt moderni quod thema dividant, quod non consueverunt antiqui. Immo est utilis praedicatori, quia divisio thematis in diversa membra praebet occasionem dilatationis in prosecutione ulteriori sermonis, Waleys.370; cf. Eiximenes.335). As in a tree the trunk grows from the root and then splits into branches, which in turn produce twigs, so in the scholastic sermon the *introductio thematis* springs from the thema, which is then divided into parts that can be further developed (Fusignano.36; Rochelle.passim; Nota.165v; Ars copiosa.17–22, where the "root" is the *introductio thematis*, see section 45-f). Similarly, as in a house, the division corresponds to the opening of the doorway (Vade.176–8).

Given this structural importance of the division, some treatises devote their entirety to it (Alcok; In predicatore), or discuss it at great length, or provide a thoughtful discussion of its history and function (Eiximenes.336–7). The longest and most detailed and inclusive discussion of the *divisio thematis* occurs in Ars copiosa.19–23v. Its chapter IV begins with a definition: "The division is the unfolding of the true meaning [of the thema] through [complete] sentences" (Diuisio est debite sentencie per orationes explicatio, 19), whose terms are then explained and illustrated.[56]

Next, Ars copiosa declares that the division can be made according to the four senses of Scripture (19v–20; cf. Schale.107v–8; Omnis.274), that is, it may simply explain and divide the literal meaning or else divide the possible allegorical, moral, or anagogical sense of the thema. For example, the thema "In the beginning God created heaven and earth" literally divided would yield something like "In this we find three things: when God created all things, who the creator is, and thirdly what he created." But the same thema may also be divided according to the verse's allegorical sense: "In these words the twofold state of human beings is shown. First the passage indicates that the state of

56 A different definition with similar explanation of its terms occurs in Omnis.274–5.

contemplatives is in heaven, when it says 'In the beginning God created heaven,' that is, men whose way of life is in heavenly things. And then it hints that the way of life of active people is in working in earthly things, when it adds 'and the earth'" (Ars copiosa.19v–20).

After this, Ars copiosa discusses the verbal means by which a division is made (20–1; cf. Ps.-Bonaventure; Higden.49–50; Omnis.276). Thus the preacher may use verb forms in the present tense, or the past, or infinitives, or the passive voice, etc. For instance, the thema "Father, I have sinned against heaven and against you" may yield the division "Here the sinner *invokes* God, *shows* his wound, *exaggerates* his sin, and *estimates* his punishment" (Ars copiosa.20). Or else, the division can be made with nouns in various grammatical cases, or with participles, and so forth. For instance, in dividing the thema "Posuit os acutum" (He has made my mouth like a sharp sword, Isa 49:2) with the help of present participles the preacher may say that "Tria hic notantur: auctoritas *dantis*, congruitas *suscipientis*, utilitas *audientis*" (Ars copiosa.21; cf. Hesse.352). Lastly, Ars copiosa deals with various modes of division, such as dividing the entire gospel or epistle lection, or the division *extra auctoritatem* and *intra auctoritatem*, both with many subdivisions and examples (21–3v). Here the author also adds a number of defects that may occur in the division (22v), such as using the same or a cognate word of that which appears in the thema, or a synonym, or something unclear (thus also in Quamvis.116). Similarly extensive discussions of the division appear in some other *artes* (see above, note 55).

The difference between *divisio extra* and *intra auctoritatem*, also discussed and illustrated at some length in Ps.-Bonaventure.8b–11a,[57] is that the *divisio extra* takes a *notion* suggested by the thema, explains it, and then divides it into parts, whereas the *divisio intra* pays close attention to the actual *words* of the thema, which it explains in some fahion. To illustrate: In dividing the thema "So run that you may obtain" (1 Cor 9:24) *extra auctoritatem*, the preacher may take the notion of "law," distinguish three kinds of law, and then apply these to his thema as follows:

> There is a threefold law: that of nature, of Scripture, and of the gospel.
> Natural law teaches what one must do;
> the law of Scripture teaches what to do and how one must act;

57 Also more briefly in Hic.158–60, saying that the *divisio* (and *subdivisio*) *exterior* may be used by "country preachers" but not by scholars.

the law of the gospel teaches what to do, how, and to what aim one must act. Therefore, the preacher of the gospel law teaches here what one must do ("run"), how one must act ("so"), and to what aim one must act ("that you may obtain"). (Ps.-Bonaventure.9a–b; cf. Higden.51)

In contrast, the same thema may be divided *intra auctoritatem* by simply analysing the words of the quoted thema, such as:

In these words we are–

invited to run ("so run"),
and stirred to strive for the prize (*bravium*; "that you may obtain").

Thus the Apostle speaks in the way of one who admonishes us to undertake a meritorious work in the first part, and in the way of one who draws us to gain the prize in the second part. (Ps.-Bonaventure.9b)

The *divisio intra* is said to be proper for a clerical audience, while the *divisio extra* is more useful for the laity (Ps.-Bonaventure.8b; Ars copiosa.21).

For the parts into which anything is divided one must find and give a logical reason. This is called *partium declaratio* by some treatises (Basevorn.275–9; Higden.50–4; Vade.176), while others use the terms *claves* and *sufficientia*. *Claves* are logical "keys" that open up the meaning of the text.[58] In the example given immediately above, such "keys" are the logical oppositions of invite vs. stir, run vs. strive for, admonish vs. draw, or merit vs. prize. Other "keys" of this sort may be time, place, and effect (Ps.-Bonaventure.9a; Higden.50). In contrast, a *sufficientia* is a rationale or reason why these particular items and their number are found in the divided word or concept (Vade.178–80; cf. Chobham.286; Dic.70; Nota.166v). Whenever a word or concept is divided into its parts, the preacher must be careful to give *all* its constituent parts.[59] Thus, the notion of "justification" must include man's contrition, God's

58 Treated at Ps.-Bonaventure.9a, 11a; Dic.69; Higden.50–4; Hic.152–4; Vade.176–8; Circa.102v–3; Nota.166v–7.

59 Notice that Ars copiosa declares that *sufficientia* is the same as *artificium*, which it discusses at great length (25v–7).

mercy, and man's satisfaction (Ars copiosa.19), or the notion of "law" must lead to neither four nor two but to three members (as above, pp. 67–8; cf. Vade.180 and Rochelle.196). *Partium declaratio* and *claves* are synonymous in Higden (parcium declaracio sive clavis, 50), while Vade in its house image calls such a *declaracio* the key (*clavis)* of the door (176). The *declaratio* can be made with the help of different word forms and their aspects, as well as by means of different "sciences," such as grammar, logic, physics, etc. (Basevorn.275–9, with many examples; Higden.50–4). This requirement of finding logical reasons applies also to further subdivisions.

The *partium declaratio* may thus lead to adding sequentially a second and even a third division (Waleys.369–70; Higden.50; Omnis.277). So does the general requirement that the division should "exhaust or express all that is contained in the thema" (Diuisio thematis debet euacuare vel exprimere totum quod in themate continetur, Hic.152). The members of the individual divisions may then be combined into longer statements.[60] An example from an actual sermon that was apparently preached to parish clergy will illustrate how the single word *Venit*, 'He came,' can lead to a complex division. The preacher begins by stating that his thema may suggest three questions: who came, to whom did he come, and what did he come for? These are answered as follows:

1. He came –
as a powerful king,
as a very wise cleric,
and as a skillful physician.

2. He came –
to prisoners without power,
to fools without wit,
and to sick people in great sorrow.

3. He came in order –
to free [men] mercifully from the devil's subjection,
to teach [men] knowingly heavenly wisdom,
and to heal [men] graciously of the poison we received from Adam.

60 Circa calls this process *subdivisio* and *combinatio* (103v).

The parts of this triple division are then combined:

> He came –
> as a powerful king to prisoners without power to free them mercifully from the devil's subjection;
> and also as a very wise cleric to fools without wit to teach them knowingly heavenly wisdom;
> and further as a skillful physician to sick people in great sorrow to heal them graciously of the poison we received from Adam.

These long sentences then form the members of the successive main parts of the sermon, where they are further developed.[61] Such multiplication of divisions is sometimes considered not a matter of logical necessity but of ornamentation (Quamvis.118: ob decorem; Waleys.369). Omnis calls the second division *exposicio*, its further expansion *ornatus*, and the combination *adaptacio* (277).

The thema can also be divided with the help of a *distinctio*, which is concerned with an individual word,[62] whereas *divisio* technically is of an entire clause or sentence (Ars copiosa.19v; Waleys.371–2; Schale.107v–8v). However, some *artes* do not always differentiate between *divisio* and *distinctio* firmly and consistently (see Chobham.266 and 284–5; Thetford.83–4; Auvergne.204; Wales.19r–v; Ad habendum.313–14; Piscario.182; Tuderto.43–6; Hesse.352).[63] This may be so because both use the same logical processes, and further, what in precise scholastic discussions is called *distinctio* derives from a much-studied and quoted text by Boethius known as *De divisione*. Another differentiation occurs in Nota, where *divisio* is distinguished from *numeracio*, the latter occurring when the preacher introduces the division of his thema not with a bridge passage but by saying, for instance, "In these words two things are indicated."[64]

---

61 The example is taken and translated from sermon W-102 (cf. Wenzel 2005a, p. 618), where the rhyming lines are given in English. Other examples of similar complexity can be found in Wenzel 1985; Wenzel 1986, ch. 3, esp. pp. 95–9; Wenzel 1994, pp. 77–8; and Horner 2006 passim.

62 Or a single notion. For example, the verse "O death, how bitter is your memory" (Ecclesiasticus 41:1) may be developed with the following distinction: "For those who love this world, the memory of death is bitter for three reasons: first because of the world they leave, second because …" (Fusignano.28–30).

63 Hesse, rather uniquely, sees the difference between *divisio* and *distinctio* in the explicit numbering of parts in the latter (355).

64 Nota.166, also with reference to Boethius (cf. *In Categorias Aristotelis*, PL 64:180).

There are several kinds of distinction, as outlined in the treatise *De divisione* by Boethius (Thetford.88 and passim; Wales.21r–v, calling it *subdivisio*; Vade.180–2; also Basevorn.292; Higden.58) or in the *Dialectica* by John Damascene (Omnis.280), which are both occasionally quoted by name. Thus, a genus may be divided into its species, a whole into its constituent parts, a word into its different meanings, and so forth. Considering a biblical word in its four senses (literal, moral, allegorical, and anagogical) is of course also a kind of *distinctio* (esp. Piscario.183; cf. Thetford.114–16; Ps.-Bonaventure; Ad habendum.315; Fusignano.58–66; Higden.35 and 65; Cordoba.345; Ps.-Aquinas.5va–6va). The discussion of *distinctio* in the *artes* thus is the point at which pulpit rhetoric touches on logic most closely; in Ars copiosa, for example, the discussion becomes almost a little treatise on distinction (24–6v). This importance of distinction and division is supported with a quotation from Porphyry: "He who divides must of necessity go through many things."[65]

As with the division, some *artes* consider how many parts a distinction may yield. Thus Cordoba says it should have at least three but no more than six (342–3) and gives examples for commonplace triads (the Trinity, the theological virtues, etc.), quaternaries (the cardinal virtues, elements, evangelists, etc.), and so on. The limited number, however, may clash with the demand of *sufficientia* (see above, p. 68) when a topic is dealt with that contains seven or more members, such as the deadly sins or other septenaries, where larger distinctions are acceptable (as illustrated in Antoninus.passim).

To set up a correct and meaningful *divisio* requires careful thought. Waleys advises in general that the preacher must weigh what is of greater and of less importance and emphasize the former (335). Hic states in simple but pithy words: "One must diligently examine the meaning of the words that appear in the thema ... These words must always be turned over and over [in one's mind] until a form appears in which the entire sense of the main thema finds expresssion, though divided and in parts" (Diligenter probanda est signacio verborum in themate positorum ... Que quidem verba semper voluenda et reuoluenda sunt donec appareat aliqua formalis in qua tota sentencia principalis thematis, licet diuisim et per partes, exprimi videatur, 150–2).

65 Porphyry, *Liber praedicabilium* 3, in Porphyry, *Isagoge sive liber V praedicabilium Aristotelis*, ed. L. Minio-Paluello, Aristoteles Latinus, 1.6–7 (Bruges / Paris, 1966), p. 12. Quoted in Ars copiosa.24 and 27v; Thetford.84; Basevorn.292; Higden.61.

Other *artes* contain similar statements (Wales.20v; Borgsleben.69), to the point of giving precise rules (Waleys.376–9; Tuderto.1–17;[66] Cordoba.337–41) or analysing various syntactic combinations contained in the thema (Rochelle). Alcok furnishes forty-five ways of dilating the sermon, most of which concern dividing a thema according to specific questions one may ask of it or with a key word applied to it.

Consequently, the preacher must determine and then restate what each and every meaningful word of his thema denotes, connotes, or implies (Alprão.325; Higden.47; Omnis.276). This is essentially a logical task in which one might go from a specific term ("just") to its genus ("the virtue of justice"), or from an effect ("mercy") to its cause ("piety"), or conversely from a cause ("wisdom") to its effect ("enlightening the mind," Cordoba.338). Ps.-Bonaventure specifies that the preacher must find out the meaning (*sententia*) and general sense (*sensus*) of his thema and to whom it is directed; if it is directed to a second person, he may distinguish between various modes of speech (Ps.-Bonaventure.8–9; see above, section 45-a, point 8, and section 45-e; cf. Exercitacio). Further, in making the division the preacher must absolutely avoid repeating the word of his thema or using a cognate, a fault which is often called *coincidencia*.[67] Likewise, a synonym[68] or, on the other hand, a word that is totally unrelated to the word in the thema will not do (Quamvis.114). Put differently, the members of the division must be distinct from or even opposite to one another, or else they will "step on each other's toes" (*conculcatio*, in Exercitacio.88rb).[69] Function words, such as *est*, prepositions, or conjunctions, can of course not be divided (Basevorn.254; Higden.21).

---

66 Tuderto begins its discussion of the division of the thema with five (uncharacteristic) ways in which the thema should be examined; they include not only considering the *perfecta latinitas* (evidently meaning the complete sense of words and syntactic structures) but also "dividing" a single term and developing the letters of a term (i.e., acrostic, 4–8).

67 Dealt with in Basevorn.273–4; Piscario.181–2; Waleys.370, 375–6; Omnis.275–6; Cordoba.338; Circa.102v; Nota.166v; Exercitacio.88rb. See also Ars copiosa. 23; Quamvis.114–16; Higden.43–4; Eiximenes.338; Vade.182–4.

68 But notice that the careful definition of Omnis declares that the division must be made *per sinonima*, "that is words that mean the same … " but not with the same words as occur in the thema (275–6).

69 But *conculcatio* is used with the meaning of multiplying of words uselessly in Piscario.198 and Nota.167.

"Among modern preachers such a division is usually made through some verbal consonance, which for earlier preachers was of no or little concern" (Apud modernos solet huiusmodi diuisio fieri per quasdam uerborum consonancias, de quibus prioribus predicatoribus nulla aut modica cura fuit, Fusignano.34). Accordingly, for many, especially later, writers of *artes* it is desirable that the terms in the members of the division run parallel to one another and rhyme (e.g., Basevorn.321–2; Fusignano.34–6; Waleys.372–6; Higden.70–1; Quamvis.118; Omnis.276–7; Alprão.325–6).

This can lead to such divisions as the following:

Like an eagle St John was –

in visu	acutissimus	per	secretorum divinorum	cognitionem;
in volatu	celerrimus	per	preceptorum divinorum	impletionem;
in gradu	sublimissimus	per	subditorum	prelationem.

The importance that such internal and end rhymes held in later medieval preaching is neatly shown by Tuderto, who now and then uses *divisio* and *rhythmus* interchangeably (e.g., 7, 28, etc.) and further gives examples of rhyming lines containing from two to ten words (72–9). In order to create such concordance in their divisions, lists of rhyming words were made available, as for instance by Geraldus de Piscario (d'Avray 1978), or preachers were advised to make their own lists (Waleys.374). Such verbal gymnastics could potentially become absurd and quite unhelpful to their audience, and this was indeed recognized by medieval authors. Eiximenes likens their practitioners to tricksters ("trufatores et histriones et uerbosi burlatores," Eiximenes.337), while Waleys defends the use of *colores rhythmici*, especially in sermons to the clergy, but condemns its excess (Waleys.372–5), as does Geraldus de Piscario after having provided several examples (Piscario.198).[70] At an earlier age, Chobham had simply rejected the use of such *ornatus sermonum* (both *similiter cadens* and *similiter desinens*), calling the latter "ridiculous" (300).

Of greater importance is the question into how many parts a thema should be divided in order to be useful to both the preacher and his audience (Ashby.28; Chobham.285–6; Thetford.86; Piscario.180–1; Fusignano.32–4; Waleys.368–9; Tuderto.16; Cordoba.341; Circa.102v;

70 For the use of rhymed divisions in vernacular sermons see Wenzel 1986, pp. 84–100.

Antoninus.V.2.end). The consensus is that three is best (strongly recommended by Basevorn.254–7 and 314), though two and four are allowed (cf. Borgsleben; Vade.180);[71] but beyond that the sermon loses its punch (Piscario.183; Fusignano.32). Yet Thomas of Todi declares that though a division into two is essential (otherwise it would not be a division), one into three is "more beautiful," and one into four is "the most beautiful" (Tuderto.16). Of course, some terms demand a division into more members, since "week," for example, may require seven (one for each day); and in a later chapter Basevorn illustrates divisions into as many as twelve members (310–13; see also Antoninus.passim).

A special concern of some *artes* is the numbering of parts. Under certain circumstances, the parts of the division should not be numbered "first, second, third" (Rochelle.196, 212; cf. Ars copiosa.19v; Ps.-Bonaventure.12a), though the introduction of the division (or the preceding bridge passage) may use a cardinal number, "two" or "three" and so on. For instance, if the thema is "[We should live] Soberly, and justly, and godly" (Titus 2:12), and the bridge passage "These words describe the perfection of a just man," the division then could be:

> But since the perfection of a just man may lie in his right ordering himself with regard to himself, to his neighbour, and to God, three things are here said, namely how one orders oneself:
>
> to oneself, in *soberly;*
> to one's neighbour, in *justly;*
> and to God, in *and godly.*
>
> But to say, "first to himself" and so on would be incorrect. (Rochelle.196)

As a general rule, the division and its terms should be short (Hic.152), and in setting it up the preacher must keep an eye on the confirmation that is to follow (Basevorn.274; Borgsleben.69–70)..If at all possible, the members of the division should follow the order of the words in the thema (Basevorn.274–5; Higden.45–6), but Omnis insists that the division must follow the order of the things signified by the words of the thema if in the biblical text they stand in a different sequence (276).

71 Vade refers here to *Ad Herennium* 1.10.17, in Ps.-Cicero, *Ad C. Herennium de ratione dicendi*, ed. Harry Caplan, Loeb Classical Library 403 (Cambridge, MA, 1961), p. 30.

Similarly, the mode of speech that appears in the thema should also be preserved in the division (Ps.-Bonaventure.8b; Higden.46–7). Higden further devotes some attention to procedures one may follow when a thema of only one or two words is to be divided into three parts (22–3, 48).

Finally, the division should be properly introduced with a "bridge passage" (see above, section 45-e). Quamvis (120) states that it would make for much elegance if one were to introduce the division with the saying of a saint or philosopher or a *manuductio* (cf. above, p. 63).

45-h Confirmation

To prove the truth of a statement – any statement – with a sentence from Scripture or another authoritative source was a basic urge in medieval thinking and writing, in preaching as much as elsewhere. Hence, the *artes praedicandi* tend to include *confirmatio* or *probatio*, and they do so under many different rubrics.[72] For instance, if in introducing the thema one were to use a syllogism, its major and minor proposition are to be proven with a Scriptural *auctoritas* (Alprão.269–98; Cordoba.334–5: for "similitudinem" read "sillogismum"). Thetford also is quite clear: "After a division has been made, it is fitting to adduce authorities for each member, so that the person who has made the division does not appear to have made the parts of his division up." Wherever something is divided, its parts must be confirmed: "Any member of a scriptural comment (*postillatio*), division, subdivision, distinction, or subdistinction must be proven with at least one authority" (Quodlibet membrum postillationis, divisionis, subdivisionis, distinctionis, subdistinctionis, ad minus una auctoritate probari debet, Hesse.356; see further below, section 45-i), to which citations in the protheme and *introductio thematis* may be added (Tuderto.44–6). Hence Basevorn can consider *confirmatio* generally as a major "ornament" of the sermon. The proof text should be a scriptural sentence or figure (Alcok.211–13, under *Historia*), though depending on what part of the sermon is to be confirmed (Ars

72 Confirmation is treated at Thetford.88; Wales.21 (*probare*); Predicacio.341, 343–4; Basevorn.279 and passim; Piscario.182–4; Dic.73; Quamvis.120; Ars copiosa. 16, 19, 27 (*probatio*); Ad erudicionem.passim; Waleys.345 and passim; Higden.54; Tuderto.22–8 (*probatio*); Hesse.356 (*autorizatio, probari*); Schale.107v, 108v; Omnis.278; Alprão.269–98, 326–7 (*probatio*); Cordoba.340–1 (*probatio*); Vade.178; Circa.103r–v; Exercitacio.89va–b; Lull.402–3 (*probatio*).

copiosa.16), it may also be a quotation from an authoritative author including canon law (Hesse.356) and even poets (Wales.21v; Alan.passim), a reasoned argument, an exemplum, a simile, word etymology, etc.

In Cicero's *De inventione*[73] and the *Rhetorica ad Herennium*,[74] *confirmatio* (together with *confutatio*) had the wider meaning of proving one's case (or disproving that of one's opponent). This wider meaning still occurs in the early *artes* by Alexander of Ashby and Thomas of Chobham (Ashby.28; Chobham.266–7 and 294–6). Ashby's definition of *confirmatio*, the third part of *sermo*, sounds exactly like what later *artes* understood by it (Diuisionem uel subdiuisionem sequatur confirmatio, in qua singula membra diuisionis confirmentur auctoritatibus uel rationibus, 28), but his further explanation clearly envisions more than a simple proof text. The same is true of Chobham, where *confirmatio et confutatio* form the fourth part of an *oratio* and are the major means of persuasion.[75]

Given this background in classical rhetoric as well as the general urge in medieval thought to prove everything, it is not surprising that *confirmatio* could be discussed under different parts of the scholastic sermon structure (for example, in Waleys). Alan includes it after making a distinction (e.g., 126), as does Cordoba (342). Yet a few later *artes*, also calling it *probatio*, deal with it specifically as a distinct part or step in the sermon structure after discussing the division (Basevorn, Tuderto, Schale, Cordoba, Higden, Omnis). In it, the parts that have been established by dividing the thema must be confirmed with an authoritative statement. In Vade confirmation is the lock (*clausura*) on the door (*ostium*) in the house which is the well-built sermon (178–80). The confirmation must contain a word that agrees with the respective word in the thema and division, if possible in sound, otherwise at least in its meaning. In other words, the confirmation must *concord* with the part that has been divided (Piscario.183–4; Quamvis.116–18). *Concordancia*, therefore, is essential to such confirmation, and many *artes* do

73 Cicero, *De inventione* 1.14.19 and 1.24.34–42.78, in Cicero, *De inventione, De optimo genere oratorum, Topica*, ed. H.M. Hubbell, Loeb Classical Library 386 (Cambridge, MA, 1976), pp. 38–40 and 68–122.

74 *Rhetorica ad Herennium* 1.10.18-17.26, in Ps.-Cicero, *Ad C. Herennium de ratione dicendi*, ed. Harry Caplan, Loeb Classical Library 403 (Cambridge, MA, 1961), pp. 32–104.

75 Other echoes of the Ciceronian confirmation and refutation occur in Si vis.29 and perhaps Ps.-Aquinas.6vb.

in fact not speak of *confirmatio* or *probatio* but of *concordancia* instead, in the sense of "concording authority" (see esp. Cordoba.340–1; Borgsleben.69–70; Exercitacio.89va and passim). Tuderto.23 uses both *probatio* and *concordancia*).

Concordancia may therefore be mentioned and discussed in the *artes* at many different places, wherever two authorities are set in relation. It includes essentially two kinds.[76] In *concordancia vocalis* two words agree in sound, that is, they share the same stem or root word; thus, *amor* can be confirmed with an authority containing such words as *amoris, amantis, amare, amatum, amandum, amando,* etc. (Ars copiosa.27; cf. Waleys.345–6). In *concordancia realis* the two words share only the same meaning; thus, if the word *cathedra* (e.g., Matthew 23:3) is divided into *cathedra presidentium, docentium,* and *iudicantium,* the first may be confirmed with *Hely sedebat super super sellam* (1 Sam 1:9, 4:13), for *sella* has the same meaning as *cathedra* (Wales.18; cf. Eiximenes.318). The best way of confirming an authority is if both kinds are present (Hic.156, considering also cases where the grammatical persons in both quotations differ; Circa.103r–v).[77] Thus Wales, which initially speaks of four kinds of preaching according to different forms of concordance, later states that "it is very fitting [for the preacher] to prove his words with authorities from Holy Scripture and say, 'On the first is written in such and such a place,' etc., so that [the two quotations] may concord in meaning and sound" (21). Schale, however, recognizes that *concordantia vocalis* may not always be possible (108v).

Ideally, a *confirmatio* should be given immediately after each part of the division or distinction. But Basevorn recognizes that many other practices are in use, including that some preachers first give the three parts and then add the respective confirmations with *pro primo scribitur,* and so on (291, which he considers *vitiosum*). One should therefore realize that *confirmatio,* like *divisio,* is in essence a logical and verbal procedure rather than merely a specific step in the sermon structure. In discussing it, a sophisticated *ars* such as Basevorn can be automatically drawn into speaking of other procedures and parts of the sermon, especially when analysing a longer illustration (e.g., at 284–91). Here and in

76 Ars copiosa speaks of three kinds of *probatio*: *ad vocem, ad rem,* and *ad intellectum* (27). Fusignano discusses the kinds of *concordancia* at some length and with helpful illustrations (40–6). Some *artes* consider as the third kind of *concordancia* the combination of the first two, i.e., *vocalis* and *realis* (Alprão.268–9).

77 In Piscario the discussion of *concordancia* is more nuanced (183–4).

other works, *confirmatio* at once leads to or in fact becomes, one way of dilating the sermon.

45-i Development (*Prosecutio*): Subdivision, Subdistinction

After the parts derived from dividing the thema have been confirmed, the preacher begins their development.[78] In some *artes,* subdivision and subdistinction are the first step toward it, while in others they form the development itself. "If you wish to build a sermon artfully (*ex arte*), choose a thema that agrees with the time and place [of your preaching] and divide it into two or three parts, whatever seems useful to you. Take the parts of the division and divide them into two or three parts, making them the members of a subdivision, and so commit the chief sections of the sermon you are to preach to memory. If you are well provided with sermon material (*si … habundans fueris in materia*), the division and subdivision of the thema is sufficient for you without further work" (Si vis.29).[79] Auvergne similarly declares that distinctions and divisions, together with interpretations and definitions, generate copious matter for the sermon (203). Even the very short In accepcione shows that the development begins with a subdivision of the respective part of the division, though without calling it thus. It should be noted, however, that in some treatises the discussion of subdivision and subdistinction is not as neatly set off or emphasized.[80] Basevorn speaks of

---

78 The development as part of the sermon structure is discussed in Chobham.266–7 (exposition through confirmation and refutation) and 272–84; Thetford (the entire treatise); Auvergne.203–9 (mostly concerned with some processes of development); Wales.19r–v, 21r–v; Predicacio.343; Basevorn.291, 295–7; Fusignano.36-94; Waleys.379–403; Higden.54–70; Quamvis.122–42; Ars copiosa.27v–9; Dic.71–3; Tuderto.29–37 (calling it *multiplicitas*); Schale.108v–11v; Omnis.278–81; Eiximenes.322, 339; Antoninus.VI.first part; Alcok (the entire treatise); Cordoba.341–8; Vade.180–4; In accepcione.31rb; Nota.167r–v; Ps.-Aquinas.3vb, 9vb; Lull.404, *multiplicatio*. Notice that some treatises deal with *dilatio* more broadly, including other parts of the sermon as well (e.g., Piscario.184–5).

79 Later Si vis considers the possibility that the preacher may not be *habundans in materia*.

80 For instance, the early Alan illustrates divisions and distinctions in the development of an authority without assigning them a separate place in the sermon structure (e.g., 114, *distinguere*; 115, *divisio*). Dic discusses sudivision immediately after division and before confirmation, though the latter term here seems to stand for the sermon development (73). Antoninus considers distinction as one way of building the entire sermon (V.3) and mentions subdivision as a way of expanding the members of the major division (V.2).

and exemplifies subdivision as one way of dilating the sermon that is more customary at Oxford (295–7).

Subdivision is the process of dividing the members of the first or main division further into two, three, four, or even more parts. "As a tree, after sprouting branches (*rami*), spreads further through twigs (*ramusculi*), so the sermon must not rest on the division of its theme" but be further developed through subdividing the members of the division and further expansion (Fusignano.36; cf. Rochelle.passim; Quamvis.122–42). The following is a very simple example: for the thema "Jesus, son of David, have pity on me" (Luke 18:38), the division is introduced with the bridge passage "This is the voice of someone asking for help," and then the main division is made, here into two parts: "He [i.e., Bartimaeus] asks Jesus; and he asks for himself." Next the first part ("He asks Jesus") is subdivided as follows:

> Regarding the first part: In this he (Bartimaeus) refers to three things (in *Jesus*):
>
> his power when he says *Jesus*, whose name means "saviour";
> his goodness when he says *son*, for *filius* derives from *philos*, which means "love";
> and his wisdom when he says *David*, for of David we read at 2 Kings 23 that *he was sitting in the chair, the wisest among three*. (Rochelle.206)

The second main part, "He asks for himself," would then be subdivided in a similar fashion. Subdivision is, therefore, different from forming sequential divisions as was demonstrated earlier, where the thema *Venit* was divided three times (above, p. 69). The resulting first part of this sequential division – "He came as a powerful king to prisoners without power to free them mercifully from the devil's subjection" – could then be subdivided into three parts if, for instance, the preacher wanted to speak of (a) the power of Christ, (b) the powerlessness of the human race, and (c) God's mercy in our redemption. In the house image of Vade, therefore, subdivision forms the three or four panes of the window (which is the division) through which light is brought into the building (180).

The considerations and rules given under "Division" apply here as well. For instance, the subdivision should have the same number of members as the major division (as they do not in the quoted example from Rochelle nor in Fusignano.36; but see Exercitacio.88va–b or Rochelle.212, which are much concerned with *conuenientia in numero*;

Ars copiosa.17v). Also, a term or notion should not be subdivided into more than four parts "lest it causes confusion in the preacher and boredom in his audience" (Ars copiosa.24). As in the main division, the members of the subdivision may or should also be confirmed with further biblical authorities.

Again, just as in the main division, what is divided can be either an entire phrase or sentence, or else a single term. Dividing the latter constitutes, technically, a *distinctio*: "Division is of an [entire] authority, distinction of a term" (Diuisio enim est auctoritatis, distinctio termini, Omnis.264).[81] Hence, in discussing the process of subdividing, some *artes* include **subdistinction** (Ars copiosa.24v–5v and passim; Hesse.354–6), although several call it simply *distinctio.* Some treatises do not verbally differentiate between division and distinction, as was noted above in section 45-g (Higden, Tuderto, Hesse).

45-j Development (*Prosecutio):* Processes of Dilatation

To subdivision and subdistinction can be added a number of other ways to dilate the sermon.[82] Omnis says that the development "begins with" subdivision and distinction and then "ends with an infinite number of modes" (278). The latter are logical or verbal procedures by which the sermon is expanded. Fusignano lists as many as twelve, which are then explained and illustrated at some length:

(1) Adding one or more authorities that agree with the respective part of the division or subdivision, or a part of it, in word form, meaning, or both.
(2) Discussing individual words.

---

81 Cordoba. 341 seems to say the same; the reading *distensio* in the edited text must be an error.

82 Discussions of ways of dilatation in addition to subdivision and subdistinction appear in Thetford (the whole treatise); Auvergne (general procedures in preaching); Ad habendum (the entire treatise); Basevorn. 291–5; Fusignano. 38–94; Dic. 71–3; Waleys. 386–402; Higden. 60–7; Tuderto. 29–37 (*multiplicatio*); Hesse. 357; Schale. 108v–11v; Omnis. 280–1; Eiximenes.322–5; Alcok (the entire treatise); Cordoba. 343–6; Hic. 158–60; Nota. 167r–v; Ps.-Aquinas. 4rb–8ra, 10va–12va (*prolongatio*). Alprão mentions a section on *processus* but does not give it; instead, it discusses ten ways of dilatation in the *introductio thematis* (269–323), including using a syllogism. For Guibert de Tournai, see above, section 10.

(3) Explaining the fourfold Scriptural senses a word can have.
(4) Defining, describing, or giving the "etymology" of a proper noun.
(5) Using degrees of comparison (e.g., *magnus, maior, maximus*) or compound words (e.g., *accepit, concepit, excepit, recepit*, etc.).
(6) Using synonyms.
(7) Developing the properties of things. For example, in dealing with the thema "The Lord has anointed you with the oil of gladness" (Ps 44:8), one may say that oil has the power to mitigate, to illumine deep water, and to make things sweet, and then apply these qualities to grace.[83]
(8) Giving examples or similes, including fables.
(9) Stating the opposite. For example, when dealing with sin, one may contrast it with grace or holiness. This procedure receives special attention in Quamvis, which calls it *impactio* (122–4, taken over in Higden.55).
(10) Dividing a whole into its parts, which seems to be the same as *subdistinctio*.
(11) Indicating causes and effects of what is said in the part to be developed.
(12) Reasoning about something said in the part, such as establishing an enthymeme, refuting an objection, and so forth.[84]

To these might be added some further devices exemplified in some *artes* or appearing frequently in actual sermons. One is a biblica *figura* or type, such as Jonah prefiguring Christ by being three days in the belly of the whale. Another common device is *excoriatio*, that is, developing the single letters of a word into phrases or sentences that begin with the same letter. For example, the noun *mors* can be unfolded into *mundi vanitas, opus carnis, rugiens leo*, and *solutio carnis*.[85] Yet another technical term used in this connection is *facies*, referring to the qualities or aspects or features or properties of what is indicated by a specific

---

83 Properties of things are already used in the early *artes* of Alan (for example, the fly, *musca*, at 122) and Chobham (274–9).

84 Chobham privileges arguments next to authorities as the main means of development or "confirmation": "ut ita quasi connexis manibus incedant ratio et auctoritas" (295).

85 Alcok.215. Other examples are MONS and TAURUS in Thetford.146, or INFERNUS and STEPHANUS in Antoninus.V.7.

word of the division or subdivision. Rochelle defines it as "any pertinent circumstance from which a moral quality may be drawn" and then lists the common *circumstantiae* with brief illustrations (200).[86] The same connection appears at greater length in Ars copiosa, which actually calls the circumstances *facies* (28). Both treatises further connect it with metaphor or metonymy (*transumptio*).[87]

Other *artes* enumerate ten (Higden; Cordoba after announcing fourteen; the same ten in Ad habendum; similarly in Alprão) or nine (Ps.-Aquinas) or eight (Thetford, Basevorn), or five (Eiximenes), or four *modi dilatandi* (Schale), but the items included are fairly much the same. Some *artes* are critical of using quotes from canon law, poetic fictions, "new prophecies," or quotes from philosophers that have no relation to morals (Eiximenes.322). Even if various treatises discuss the same devices, the form of their doing so can be quite different. Some treatises build up a logical system with its own divisions and subdivisions (Waleys, Eiximenes), while others treat various modes of expansion more casually (Chobham). For example, Tuderto illustrates various devices by applying them to one and the same thema, whereas Schale similarly illustrates three of the four announced modes of amplification by applying them to the three members of the same divided thema. The forty-five words that Alcok lists and illustrates as aids in dividing the thema can also serve "to multiply the subject matter and expand it in any main or other part of the sermon" (206), a claim that Alcok repeats when treating circumstances, biblical figures and narrations, and definitions in particular.

A curious and apparently unique piece of instruction on generating the sermon matter appears in Eiximenes:

> When you want to examine the preaching matter, you should place the

86 The "circumstances" form a major topic in classical and medieval rhetoric as well as in moral theology, especially in hearing confession; see for instance Higden.45. They are usually listed in a hexameter: "Quis, quid, ubi, quibus auxiliis, cur, quomodo, quando." See Gründel 1963.

87 "Octauus modus dilatandi est facies, nam facies in hoc loco transumptio vocatur, uel facies in hoc loco dicitur omnis conueniencia ex qua potest moralitas elici ... Et nota quod septem sunt facies ex quibus potest moralitas in sermone elici habundanter" (28). The use of this term in preaching seems to go back to William of Auvergne, *De faciebus mundi*; see above, section 8.

> thema or the matter you want to preach about, as it were, in the centre of a circle, and then around it arrange in order the Ten Commandments, the articles of the faith, the gifts of the Holy Spirit, the eight beatitudes, the five bodily senses, the seven works of mercy, the seven virtues, and the seven vices. And then relate the matter you want to preach about in due order with some distinction concerning the material mentioned according to whether they agree with each other or are opposite to each other, or according to something relevant that comes to your mind, until you have enough material for the sermon. (323)

This "preaching wheel" is reminiscent of the depiction of five or more septenaries on rolls that were used in scholastic schoolrooms.[88]

Finally, in dealing with the development of the sermon some treatises discuss **the order of development,** that is, the order in which the parts that have been established by division and subdivision may be combined and/or further developed. For example, if a thema has been divided into three parts (1-2-3), and each part further into three (a-b-c, d-e-f, g-h-i), the latter subparts can be developed in their simple order from a to i. But one can also combine and then develop a-d-g, b-e-h, c-f-i. Basevorn calls this entire "ornament" *correspondentia* (299–300; a similar discussion of *connexio membrorum* in Exercitacio.89rb). Basevorn then adds such similar structural tricks as *circulatio* (combining g and b, etc.) and *convolutio* (having a, d, and g agree with each other). Other rhetorical tricks of this kind consist in further dividing the subdivisions, leading to twenty-seven members; or in subdividing 1 into three, 2 into two, and 3 not at all, in which case the sermon would structurally look like a pyramid (Quamvis.130, and Higden.57; both then speak similarly of sermons that look like a line, a plane, or a cube). Quamvis adds further that it would be even more elegant or refined (*curiosius*) if one could show that what is stated in the parts follows some natural or logical progression; for instance, in dividing "good" into three kinds: that of nature, of grace, and of glory, one can show that the second presupposes the first, and the third both the first and the second (134).

---

88 Such scrolls bear diagrams of sacred history as well as wheels of septenaries. See Henry 1990, p. 101, with references to earlier studies. A different kind of "preaching machine," with a *figura* and circles, is described in Lull (see above, section 43).

However, the anonymous author then adds that "I consider it foolish to spend a lot of effort on such curiosities" (Fatuum tamen reputo circa tales curiositates studere, 134).

In connection with the progressive development of the announced parts, some *artes* also reflect briefly on making a **digression**, which according to Gregory the Great is permissible if it serves the preacher's main purposes (Basevorn.297–8; cf. Chobham.266; Fusignano.42–4; Waleys.356; Hesse.357).[89] Some *artes* condemn it (Thetford.110; Ps.-Bonaventure.16b), while conversely Ars copiosa and Higden list it among the modes of dilatation (Ars copiosa.27v; Higden.66, the edited text should read *digressionem*).

45-k Combination of the Parts (*Unitio*)

Basevorn considers it especially elegant if the preacher can find a single authority which, at the end of his sermon, would combine the members of the main division and thereby "tie up"[90] the entire process of the sermon. It calls this process *unitio*, "a phrase or sentence that contains united what has been said separately in the development," that is, "all the words that have been developed in the sermon" (306–7; similarly Quamvis.132; Schale.111v). In the house image of Vade this final combination forms the roof, which is nothing other than a combination or composition of tiles or of straw or of some other covering with which the house is finally completed. In the same way, in a sermon or collation there must be some gluing or chaining together [*conglutinatio et conchatenatio*] of what has been said before, and in this way the work one has begun will be finished in perfection (184–6).[91]

This process of combining members by means of a single (new) proof text (*connexio, combinatio*, or *colligatio partium*)[92] may of course occur

89 Gregory, *Moralia*, prologue (PL 75:415). The passage is quoted in support of the orderly structure of the sermon in Basevorn.235 and 297, and Fusignano.42–4.

90 Hence some vernacular sermons speak of "the knot" of the sermon; see Wenzel 1976, pp. 155–60. Both *colligere* (to gather) and *colligare* (to tie up) are used in Quamvis.

91 Such a final combination could of course also be made without a unifying authority (e.g. Ashby.31; Chobham.303; Lull.399: *recolligere et recapitulare*).

92 But notice that the terms *connexio* or *colligatio* are also used for the linking of proof texts (as in Waleys.386–90, various reasons for *connexio vel colligatio auctoritatum)* or for the order in which parts of a division or subdivision are combined in the development (see above, p. 83); thus in Circa.104; Exercitacio.88vb–9va; Ad erudicionem.40v; Ars copiosa.16 and 29 seems to fuse or confuse the two.

in other parts of the sermons as well, as can be seen in the sample sermon below (sections 46–7).[93]

45-1 Closing Formula

Several *artes* specify how the sermon is to be ended.[94] Some mention it only in passing, while others devote an entire paragraph (Ashby, Schale) or even section to it (Basevorn, calling it uniquely *clausio*). *Conclusio* or *epilogus* had been part of a speech in classical rhetoric, comprising recapitulation, admonition, and prayer (*oratio*),[95] and reappears thus in Ashby. Chobham expands on this: the conclusion becomes the sixth and final part of an oration, where "what has been said is briefly recapitulated so as to be better kept in one's memory," and then continues: "Preachers add at the end of their preaching a small part that is not in [classical] rhetoric, namely a prayer to God that through hearing what has been said and acting, their audience may come to the kingdom of heaven" (267–8), points which are repeated later and supported with a reference to St Paul's practice of concluding his epistles with a prayer (303). Basevorn praises such a *clausio* because it links the end of the sermon to its beginning, and it exemplifies "directing the mind to God" with a variety of cases (praise, detesting what is evil, desiring what is good) which finish with such formulas as "To whom be honour and glory"or "Which he may grant who lives and reigns forever," and the like, formulas that are ubiquitous in actual sermons. They always end with an "Amen," which Waleys states is usually said by the congregation (ad quam consueverunt auditores respondere "Amen," 403). A slightly different formula is offered by Fusignano: the preacher must "conclude his sermon with a prayer in which he asks God for grace in the present and glory in the future" (16), again a formula one finds

93 Other examples of final *unitio* from actual sermons can be found in Wenzel 2008a, pp. 281–2; Wenzel 2008b, p. 77.

94 Ashby.31; Chobham.267–8 and 303; Basevorn.307–10; Fusignano.16; Ars copiosa.29; Waleys.403; Higden.58; Tuderto.38–9; Schale.111v; Hic.158; Si vis.30.

95 *De inventione* 1.52.98, in Cicero, *De inventione, De optimo genere oratorum, Topica*, ed. H.M. Hubbell, Loeb Classical Library 386 (Cambridge, MA, 1976), p, 146; *Ad Herennium* 1.3.4, in Ps.-Cicero, *Ad C. Herennium de ratione dicendi*, ed. Harry Caplan, Loeb Classical Library 403 (Cambridge, MA, 1961), p. 8. For the three parts see *Ad Herennium* 2.30.47, though with different terms (p. 144); differently in *De inventione* 1.52.98 (p. 146).

in many sermon collections. Ars copiosa suggests the same formula together with a brief recapitulation of the sermon's main points; thus, if the preacher had been speaking of faith and justice, he may conclude with "We therefore ask God that he grant us to keep this faith and justice in such a way in the present that we may be able to come to future glory" (Rogamus ergo Dominum ut hanc fidem et iusticiam nos seruare concedat taliter in presenti ut ad futuram gloriam pertingere valeamus, 29; similarly Basevorn.308 and Tuderto.39).

PART III

Sample Sermon

46 Text

That the structural elements surveyed in the preceding chapters were in fact used by late-medieval preachers can be shown by analysing an extant sermon text. For this I have chosen a sermon preached at the visitation of a monastic community, which has been preserved in a unique copy in Worcester, Cathedral Library, MS F.10, fols 248vb–50va (sermon W-130 in Wenzel 2005a). The text is very rich in its rhetorical structure. It is also faulty, in that it contains a number of evident errors, most likely made by the scribe, and thereby will demonstrate how readers and editors of medieval sermons can be helped by a thorough understanding of the scholastic sermon structure. I have reproduced it as it appears in the manuscript and have supplied in the notes suggested correct readings as well as what sources I have been able to identify. Interlinear material appears between slashes (\/), marginal additions between angle brackets (<>). I have further added structural markers boldfaced in square brackets in the text, which are then explained in the following section 47. A translation of the sermon can be found in Wenzel 2008b, pp. 270–82.

[f. 248vb]

[a] *Videamus si floruerit vinea*, Canticorum 7º capitulo.[96]

[b] Reuerendi patres ac domini, in predicatore verbi Dei tria specialiter requiruntur, scilicet sapiencia, sermonis complacencia, et uirtuosa potencia siue gracia. Sapiencia enim in predicatore requiritur vt assistentes doceat; conplacencia vt audientes alliciat; et uirtuosa potencia siue gracia ut ascultantes a malo ad bonum effectualiter reuocet et reducat. Propter que tria eciam cum necessarium sit vt scilicet existat facundus et eloquens, quia secundum Augustinum libro 4º *De doctrina Christiana,* capitulo xiº, "eloquens debet ita loqui vt doceat" per suam sapienciam, "vt delectet" per sermonis complacenciam, "et vt flectat" per uirtuosam potenciam siue graciam. Et subdit consequenter ibidem: "Docere necessitatis est, delectare suauitatis, flectere vero victorie."[97]

Verum quia ideo michi verbum Dei prenunciaturo [f. 249ra] ista prelibata deficiunt, compellor clamare ad Dominum et dicere cum

96 Canticles 7:12. The Vulgate reads *floruit*; the scribe first wrote the same and then "corrected" it to *floruerit* by interlinear insertion.

97 See Augustine, *De doctrina* 4.12.27, in Augustine, *De doctrina Christiana*, ed. and trans. R.P.H. Green (Oxford, 1995), p. 228; cf. Cicero, *Brutus* 185, in Cicero, *Brutus*, ed. E. Malcovati (Leipzig, 1970), p. 55.

propheta, *A, a, a, Domine Deus, nescio loqui, quia puer ego sum*, Jeremie primo capitulo.[98] In qua auctoritate quoad me triplex defectus annotatur. Ecce enim primo notatur defectus sciencie, quia *nescio*; secundo in me notatur defectus verbalis complacencie, quia *nescio loqui*; tercio in me notatur defectus virtuose potencie, quia *puer ego sum*. Vnde proprie infirmitatis et \in/sufficiencie conscius aliud refugium non inuenio nisi ponere totaliter spem meam in Deo meo qui Moysen seruum suum mittendum ad populum in Egipto et excusantem se eo quod non fuerat eloquens, vt patet Exodi 4° capitulo, benignus animauit eum dicens sibi illud quod sequitur ibidem eodem capitulo: *Quis fecit os hominis, aut quis fabricatus est surdum et mutum, uidentem et cecum et audientem? Nonne ego? Perge igitur, ego ero in ore tuo doceboque te et loquaris.*[99] **[c]** Ipsum igitur in huius collacionis exordio inuoco et exoro quatinus ipse qui fabricatus est surdum et mutum mecum sit in hoc opere michi uirtuosam potenciam tribuendo, sitque in ore meo michi sermonis complacenciam largiendo, et doceat me quid loquar michi sapienciam infundendo. Et recommendo deuotis oracionibus vestris, etc.

[d] *Videamus si floruit vinea*, vbi supra.

[f] Celestis quidem agricola, metrum et mensura[100] tocius ordinis sublunaris et etheree mansionis, a luce prima in vesperam sue fabrice influens incrementa, vineam quandam electam in loco vberi, sanctam scilicet religionem monasticam, in vitibus sanctorum patrum nostrorum primo in Egipti partibus plantatam ad horam, quam postea ab inimici lupi rapacitate sua dextera adquisitam in tocius Christianissimi[101] terminos transtulit et transduxit.[102] Cuius vinee monastice plantule terram orti[103] militantis ecclesie sic firmarunt quod pre ceteris aliis religionibus in vitibus viret, in palmitibus floret, in botris fructificat incessanter, ligatur frequencius per funes obediencie, purgatur diligencius per abdicacionem proprietatis, foditur profundius per mortificacionem carnis proprie, et propagatur per salutaria statuta et consilia. Ideo in nostro visitacionis exordio diligenter inquiramus et sic *si* presens *vinea floruerit videamus*. Videamus si sufficientibus palmitibus complantetur,

98 Jeremiah 1:6.

99 Exodus 4:11–12.

100 Derived from Aristotle, *Metaphysics* 10 (1052b.32); cf. *Auctoritates Aristotelis* 1.239 (Hamesse 1974, p. 135).

101 Read *Christianismi*.

102 The preacher has Psalm 79 in mind, here verse 9, later verse 14, at [j.1a].

103 Frequent medieval spelling for *horti* (from *hortus*, "garden").

plantata debitis sepibus minuatur,[104] munita a cultore vinee diligencius expurgetur, expurgata a custodi[105] vigili vindemietur, et a lupine rabiei insultibus preseruetur, vt in tempore suo fructibus copiosis exuberet, vbi prius forte flores minime pullularunt. Idcirco primitus exquisita diligencia *videamus si floruerit vinea.*

[g.1] In quibus verbis breuiter patent tria:

labor sollicite visitacionis, ibi *videamus;*
decor monastice congregacionis, ibi *vinea;*
et odor honeste conuersacionis, in *floruerit.*

Si floruerit –

labor sollicite visitacionis, circa statum fraternum, debet diligencius inuigilare vt *uideamus;*
decor monastice congregacionis ad fructum producendum, debet vberius germinare, in *vinea;*
et odor honeste conuersacionis quoad bonum exemplum, debet se diffusius dilatare, *si floruerit.*

[h.1] Pro primo scribitur Genesis 37 capitulo: *Vide in Sichemis* (vel *Sichem*) *si cuncta sint prospera erga fratres tuos et renuncia michi.*[106] Sichen enim interpretatur, etc.[107] Pro secundo scribitur Canticorum 2° capitulo: *Vinee florentes odorem dederunt.*[108] Et sic, ut labor finiatur, *videamus* vt decor cognoscatur *in vinea* et odor percipiatur in flore [f. 249rb] *si floruit;* aggrediamur nostri officii primordia et *videamus si floruit.*

[g.2] Sed pro ulteriori processu istius collacionis exilis est breuiter aduertendum quod hec vinea religiosa –

est munienda sepibus, scilicet officiariis,
et actiue plantanda seu dilatanda palmitibus uirtuosis, claustralibus scilicet conplatiuis,[109]

---

104 Read *muniatur.*
105 Read *custode.*
106 Genesis 37:14.
107 *Sichem* is usually said to mean *labor,* "work."
108 Canticles 2:13.
109 Read *contemplatiuis.*

et tercio ipsa est purganda viciosis putredinibus a prelatis et visitatoribus inquisitis.

Et ideo debet florere in contemplatiuis per obidiencie promptitudinem, per vite sanctitatem, et per regularis discipline debitam consideracionem, per sufficientem in necessariis releuacionem, et per discretam in corrigendis excessibus reformacionem.

Et sic –

in actiuis debet virere,
in contemplatiuis florere,
et in prelatis debet iugiter redolere.

Et ideo non precipitanter et premature, non ignoranter et indebite, sed diligenter et discrete huius visitacionis exequendo officia debita *videamus si floruit vinea.*

[j.1]

[i.1] Dixi primo et principaliter an vinea munienda sepibus, scilicet officiariis actiuis, floreat, in eis –

per honestam conuersacionem,
per fidelem administracionem,
et per feruidam deuocionem.

[j.1a] Nam mundo totaliter posito in maligno auaricie sator ipse malicie, *aper de silua,*[110] vineam nostram, religionem scilicet monasticam, in suis bonis operibus temporalibus eterminare [111] nititur et eciam demoliri. Que nisi quibusdam officiariis circumspectis et prouidis quasi sepibus muniatur, rapax manus mundi furto armato nedum bona huius vinee in foliis et ramusculis auferet set eciam substanciam viuendi tolleret in radice. Debetis ergo vos officiarii hanc vineam sepiendo inimicos Christi et Ecclesie expellere velut spine et prudenter contra vulpinam fraudem vestrorum inimicorum laqueos et machinas quantum expedit tendere, expandere, et parare vobis. Igitur dicimus vestras pulsando memorias, *Capite vobis vulpeculas paruulas que demolliuntur*

110 Psalm 79:14
111 Read *exterminare.*

vineas, Canticorum 2° capitulo.[112] Secundum enim Philosophum XII *De animalibus*, odor florentis vinee et fructificantis omnibus venenosis animalibus contrariatur, et ideo ipsa florente et fructificante fugiunt colubri et bufones sustinere eius fragranciam non ualentes.[113] Sic reuera officiarii sancti et deuoti, si in seculo floreant per mundiciam conuersacionis in moribus, si fructificent per honestatem religionis in extrincesis[114] actibus, cessabit vtique lingua fellica obloqui, peruersa fugiet coluber scandali, et odor fame suauissime redolebit, vt sic tandem illud quod scribitur Ecclesiastici 24° capitulo dicere possit talis officiarius: *Ego quasi vitis fructificaui suauitatem odoris et flores mei fructus honoris et honestatis*.[115] De hiis enim diligencius inquiramus et *si* presens *vinea floruit videamus*.

[j.1b] Secundo dixi quod videre volumus si vinea hec religiosa floreat in officiariis per fidelem administracionem. Scribit enim auctor *De proprietatibus rerum* quod vinea plantata in terra humida siue pingui luxuriat in ramos et folia, nec flores nec fructus germinat nisi raro.[116] Sic dum nostri officiarii situantur in nimia pinguedine cupiditatis terrene vel in nimia humiditate carnalis voluptatis et petulancie, tunc in voto voluntarie paupertatis non fructificat[117] neque floret, set in prohibitis virescit, ymmo cum Achor qui *pallium coccineum valde bonum* [f. 249va] *et ducentos siclos argenti regulam et auream* cum \de/ anathemate Iericho abstulit et eciam abscondit,[118] et cum Anania et Saphira vetida[119] tunc occultat,[120] et tandem cum ficu fatua florente folia et non fructum diuinam suscipit vlcionem.[121] Debet enim officiarius quoad alios iusticie facere equitatem, quoad seipsum debet habere vite asperitatem, et quoad suum officium faciet vbertatem. Vnde Psalmo 11° sic loquitur propheta: *Iustus vt palma florebit*.[122] In palma, secundum Augustinum

---

112 Canticles 2:15.

113 Cf. Bartholomaeus Anglicus, *De proprietatibus* 17, "De vinea," in Bartholomaeus Anglicus, *De proprietatibus rerum* (Nuremberg, 1482), n.p.

114 Read *extrinsecis*.

115 Ecclesiasticus 24:23.

116 Bartholomaeus, *De proprietatibus* 17, "De vinea."

117 The scribe wrote singular verbs here and in the following clause (on Ananias), evidently taking them to refer to *vinea* rather than the persons mentioned.

118 Joshua 7:21 and context.

119 Read *vendita*.

120 Cf. Acts 5:1 ff.

121 Cf. Mark 11:12–21.

122 Psalm 91:13.

ibidem, reperire possimus[123] asperitatem in cortice, pulchritudinem in ramis, et vberimos fructus in arboris summitate.[124] Vnde talibus officiariis dicit Christus Mathei 24°: *Ite et vos in vineam meam,*[125] ite scilicet fideliter administrando, aspere conuersando, et vberrime fructificando. Et quia inquirere volumus an iam sit ita, *videamus si floruit vinea.*

[j.1c] Dixi tercio quod videre volumus si floreat in officiariis hec vinea religiosa per feruidam religionem[126] deuocionem. Dicit enim Albertus quod vinea bene fructificat ac floret in calida terra et arida.[127] Pariformiter, si officiarius floreat per deuocionis caliditatem, marcescat per voluptatis ariditatem, et lucescat per caritatis fructificacionem, tunc satis euidet quod talis in vinea sua floret, vt dicere valeat illud Canticorum 2° capitulo: *Ego flos campi et lilium conuallium.*[128] Flos enim campi, secundum Auicennam, est gracilis in stipite, rubicundus in colore (quia sanguinea redemitus), et quia[129] foliis perornatur.[130] Sic debet vir religiosus esse flexibilis in stipite humilitatis, rubicundus in deuocione feruide caritatis, et in foliis quinque sensuum meritorie perornatus. Et sicud[131] conuallium, quod crescit naturaliter inter petras, illesum tamen permanet inter eas, ita talis, licet cum scolaribus debeat multociens communicare, eis[132] tamen deuocionis florem mundi duricia ledere non valebit.

[k.1] Tunc enim potest dicere visitator diligens et sollicitus illud Canticorum 6 capitulo: *Descende in ortum meum vt viderem poma conuallium et inspicerem si floruisset vinea et germinasset mala punica.*[133] *Descende*

123 Probably read *possumus.* The scribe of this sermon several times writes *u* for *i* and the reverse; see below at note 150.

124 Cf. Augustine, *Enarrationes*, at 91.13, in PL 37:1179; and Hugh of Folieto, *De bestiis* 1.22, in PL 177:24; Alan of Lille, *Distinctiones dictionum theologicalium,* in PL 210:888–9, and others.

125 Matthew 20:4 and 7.

126 Read *religionis.*

127 Perhaps Albertus, *De vegetabilibus* 5.1.8 and 6.1.35 in Albertus Magnus, *De vegetabilibus libri vii,* ed Ernst Meyer and Karl Jessen (Berlin, 1867), pp. 320 and 462–3.

128 Canticles 2:1.

129 The context requires *quinque.*

130 Cf. Bartholomaeus, *De proprietatibus* 17, "Flores," in Bartholomaeus Anglicus, *De proprietatibus rerum* (Nuremberg, 1482), n.p.

131 Add *lilium.*

132 Read *eius.*

133 Canticles 6:10. The Vulgate text reads: *Descendi ad hortum nucum ut viderem ...*

iuxta[134] *in ortum,* inquam in ortum istius visitacionis, *vt viderem poma conuallium,* idest officiariorum, quantum ad honestam conuersacionem quoad primum; *et inspicerem* si floruissent vinee per fidelem administracionem quoad secundum; *et germinassent mala punica* per feruidam deuocionem quoad tercium. Et[135] inquiramus cercius ista tria, *videamus si floruit vinea.*

In quibus uerbis innuitur visitancium diligencia cum dicitur *uideamus;* secundo annectitur actiuorum excrescencia in *vinea;* et tercio adiungitur contemplatiuorum complacencia cum subinfertur *floruit.*

[j.2]

Dixi secundo principaliter quod uidere volumus an hec vinea floruit per regularis discipline studiositatem.

[j.2a] Docet enim experiencia cottidiana quod staturam humilem habet vitis, et quanto plus floribus, botris, et fructibus honoretur,[136] eo magis flexibilior et totam ad yma profundius se inclinat. Ita est enim de bonis religiosis. Quanto magis uirtutum carismatibus polleant, tanto sunt ad obediendum proniores et ad se humiliandum suis superioribus prompciores. In[137] verus obediens verissime comprobatur. Vnde beatus Bernardus in quodam sermone de sancto Andrea de ista materia notabiliter scribit per hunc modum: "Perfectus obediens moram nescit, vt scilicet mandatum non imperantis."[138] [f. 249vb] Vnde primo precepta euangelica et alia ad que astringimur, deinde iussa superiorum nostrorum in omnibus licitis et honestis effectualiter impleamus, vt vere dicere possimus id quod scribitur Exodi 24 capitulo: *Omnia que locutus est Dominus faciemus et erimus obedientes.*[139] Docet enim auctor *De naturis* quod lilia aquatica et eciam solsequia sole oriente aperiunt folia sua, ipso vero occidente folia sua claudunt, et in hoc solis aspectibus se

---

134 Scribal mistake for *inquam,* here anticipated; or else the words *iuxta in ortum* may have been cancelled by underlining.

135 Add *ut.*

136 For *oneretur,* "is burdened."

137 A word like *humilitate* seems to be missing. It is also possible that *verus* was to be followed by *religiosus.*

138 Apparently a garbled passage. In his second sermon on the nativity of St Andrew, Bernard discusses "perfectae obedientiae formam," but closer to this sermon text is his *De diversis,* sermon 41.7: "Fidelis obediens nescit moras ... ut imperantis colligat voluntatem," see *Sancti Bernardi Opera,* ed. Jean Leclercq, C.H. Talbot, and H.M. Rochais, vol. 5 (Rome, 1968), p. 434, and vol. 6.1 (Rome, 1970), p. 249.

139 Exodus 24:7.

conformant.[140] Et sic conformiter precipiente prelato verus religiosus in complecione operis omnes vires animi aperiret et ipso prohibente voluntatem transgrediendi clauderet, suo prelato in singulis obtemperando. Vt sicut per obediencie promptitudinem floreat *quasi ros rosarum in diebus vernis, et quasi lilia que sunt in transitu aquarum*, Ecclesiastici 54 capitulo.[141] Et quia inquirere volumus de claustralium obediencia, *videamus si floruit vinea* in eis.

[j.2b] Hec[142] vinea religiosa per vite sanctitatem et innocencie puritatem. Refert enim doctor \De Lira/ super librum Numerorum quod Salomonis ministri habebant vestes floribus diuersis distinctas secundum diuersa officia, ex quibus statim cognoscebatur officium cuiuslibet ministri.[143] Reuera quicquid in claustralibus interius[144] in obediencia et humilitate, exterius florere debet in exemplaris operis puritate, et sic nedum per humilitatem sibi proficiant sed eciam per exteriorem sanctimonie suo proximo splendeant puritatem. Dicit enim Paladius *De agricultura* quod amigdalus diligenter culta et in vinea contemplata[145] plus fructificat quam in ortis aliis vel in campis. Nam secundum Ysidorum ipsa cunctis arboribus fecundius floret.[146] Sic procul dubio claustralis ortus regulis obseruancie sarculis circumfossus in offerendo suiipsius arborem cum radice placidiores Deo fructus profert et germinat quam in mundo et primicias placacionis in floribus sancte conuersacionis exhibet Deo suo. Vnde de tali scribitur Ecclesiaste vltimo capitulo: *Florebit amigdalus*, supple in sanctimonie puritate, *et inpinguabitur locusta*, in boni operis exemplacione.[147] Sic enim *de fructu manuum suarum plantauit vineam*, Prouerbiorum vltimo capitulo.[148] Et ideo in claustralium puritate et sanctimonia *videamus si floruit vinea*.

140 Pliny, *Historia naturalis* 2.41.109; 18.67.252; 22.29.57, in Pliny, *Natural History*, ed. Harris Rackham et al., 10 vols, Loeb Classical Library 330 etc. (Cambridge, MA, 1938–63), 1:250, 5:348, and 6:332. Cf. Isidore, *Etymologiae* 17.9.37, in Isidore of Seville, *Etymologiarum sive originum libri xx*, ed. W.M. Lindsay, 2 vols, Oxford Classical Texts (Oxford, 1911), n.p.

141 Ecclesiasticus 50:8.

142 The beginning of this part is garbled again. One would expect something like: "Dixi secundo quod videre volumus si hec vinea religiosa floruit ..."

143 Cf. Lyra, *Postilla*, on Exodus [!] 28, in Nicholas of Lyra, *Postilla super totam Bibliam* (Venice, 1488), n.p.

144 A verb is missing, perhaps *est*.

145 Read *complantata*?

146 Cf. Isidore, *Etymologiae* 17.7.24, with *prior* instead of *fecundius*.

147 Ecclesiastes 12:5.

148 Proverbs 31:16.

[j.2c] Dixi tercio quod videre volumus si floruit in contemplatiuis hec vinea per regularis discipline studiositatem. Olym namque claustrales senes cum iunioribus vineas et vites librorum propriis manibus conscripserunt. Scribebant nonnulli codices plures inter horas canonicas interuallis captatis, et tempora pro quiete corpori commendata fabricandis codicibus concesserunt. De quorum laboribus vsque in hodiernum diem in plerisque splendent monasteriis aliqua sacra gazophilacia diuersis libris plena ad dandam scienciam salutis studere volentibus atque lumen delectabilem semitis aliorum. O felix prouidencia pro futuris infinitis posteris valitura, cui virgultorum nulla plantacio, nulla frugum seminacio comparatur nec aliqua multitudo quorumlibet armentorum! Hii fuerunt suis temporibus vulpium <spiritualium> venatores [f. 250ra] robustissimi, qui iam aliis sua recia reliquerunt vt prauas vulpeculas que non cessant florentes religionis nostre vineas demoliri. Sed prothdolor, sicut iam fertur:

Liber Bachus respicitur et in ventrem trahicitur,
liber codex despicitur et a manu eicitur,

sicque calicibus epotandis non codicibus emendandis indulget hodie studium plurimorum, sic relinquitur studii vinea desolata quasi alter ager hominis pigri et quasi altera vinea viri stulti.[149] Iob 15 scribitur: *Manus eius arescent, ledetur quasi hominis vinea in primo flore botris*[150] *eius, et quasi oliua proiciens florem suum.*[151]

Non sic, reuerendi mei, sed sicud dicit Sapiens Ecclesiastici 39 capitulo: *Florete flores quasi lilium, date odorem et florete in graciam et collaudate canticum et benedicite Dominum in omnibus operibus suis.*[152] Lilia enim pallent in radicibus, candent in foliis, virent in foliis, et redolent in humoribus atque granis. Sic enim claustrales –

psallerent[153] in fructuosa sacre scripture recitacione,
virerent in librorum composicione,
et redolerent in sciencie adquisicione,

149 Cf. Proverbs 24:30.
150 Read *botrus*; cf. note 123 above.
151 Job 15:32–3.
152 Ecclesiasticus 39:19.
153 Read *pallerent*, as required by context, though *psallerent* makes sense in connection with *recitacione*.

[k.2] vt de eis verificetur illud Ezichielis 17 capitulo: *Facta est vinea et fructificauit in palmites et emisit propagines.*[154]

Facta est vinea, scilicet virens per obediencie promptitudinem, quoad primum;
fructificauit in palmites, scilicet candens per vite sanctitatem, quoad secundum;
et emisit propagines, redolens per discipline studiositatem, quoad tercium.

Idcirco vigilanti solercia *videamus si floruit vinea*. Ecce speculatorum operacio, *videamus*; ecce claustralium inhabitacio, *vinea*; et ecce bonorum morum germinacio in flore, *si floruit*.

[j.3]

[i.3] Dixi tercio principaliter, et breuius, quod videre volumus si floreat hec vinea religiosa in prelatis –

per sollicitam subditorum consideracionem,
per sufficientem in necessariis releuacionem,
et per discretam in corrigendis defectibus reformacionem.

Quoad primum oportet quod diligencius excolatur; quoad secundum vt sepius visitetur; et quoad tercium vt superfluis expurgetur.

[j.3a] Debet enim prelatus circumspeccione prouida et prouidencia circumscripta[155] vineam sue cultvre locatam excolere diligenter irrigando arida, amputando putrida, et inualida releuando. Arentes debet erigere zelo singulari, delinquentes debet corrigere modo regulari. Corrigat ergo delinquentes flagello discipline, reficiat ignaros pabulo doctrine, et protegat innocentes a dampno ruine. Et sic prerupta conglutinet, torta rectificet, et tumultuosa rite pacificet cum quiete. Vnde sibi precipitur tanquam angelo Apocalipsis 14 capitulo: *Mitte falcem tuam acutam et vindemia botros vinee terre quoniam mature sunt uve eius.*[156] Et vindimiatur vinea terre quando prelati mature ipsam deuocius excolendo per solicitam in subditis consideracionem amplexari festinant. Nichilominus adhuc quoad alia *videamus si floruit vinea*.

154 Ezekiel 17:6.
155 Read *circumspecta*.
156 Revelation 14:18.

[j.3b] Dixi eciam quod videre volumus si in prelatis floreat hec vinea per sufficientem in necessariis releuacionem. Vnde de prelato scribitur Canticorum primo capitulo: *Botrus cipri dilectus meus michi in vineis.*[157] Semen cypri secundum naturales est candidum et odoriferum, quod si oleo coctum fuerit [f. 250rb] fit inde vnguentum deliciosum confortatiuum, ac eciam restauratiuum. Sic enim debet diligencia prelati suo conferre vnguento pii auxilii et confortacionis collirium, vt scilicet circa bene versantes non vtatur cauterio sed vnguento, non emplaustro corosiuo set pocius electuario confortatiuo. Vnde sibi precipit Christus, Mathei 21 capitulo: *Fili, vade operari in vinea mea*[158] – *fili* scilicet per imitacionem, *vade* ad pietatem, et *operari* per salutiferam in necessariis releuacionem. Et ad hoc excitat deuocio pia vt *videamus si floruit vinea.*

[j.3c] Dixi tercio, et est finis, quod videre volumus si floreat in prelatis hec vinea religiosa per discretam in corrigendis defectibus reformacionem. Nam plures profecto imfirmos allicit regularis obseruancie iuga subeunda mansuetudo compassionis quam ferrum vel gladius austeritatis. Et verum si prelatus ad intima proprie infirmitatis pectoralia se transferat, tunc ad corrigendum aliorum defectus micior apparebit. De ista materia cauetur in canone XV distinccione, capitulo *Licet,* et capitulo *Disciplina,* et capitulo *Recedite;* et L distinccione, capitulo *Ponderet.*[159] Ideo circa subditos inesse debet prelatus[160] et iuste consulens misericordia et pie seuiens disciplina. Hinc est quod semiuiuo adhibetur vinum et oleum, vt per vinum purgentur <vulnera> putrida et per oleum suauiter dimulceantur nimio dolore sauciata. Prelatus ergo in vino morsum districcionis adhibeat, in oleo moliciem pietatis benigne admisceat. Ergo lenitas cum seueritate facienda est, vt ex vtroque quoddam tempamentum[161] debite proporcionatum resultet, vt neque multa asperitate vlcerentur subditi neque nimia benignitate soluantur. Sic enim iuste iudicando stateram in manu gestat prelatus, in vtroque penso iusticiam et misericordiam portet, vt iusto libramine quedam per equitatem corrigat, quedam vero per miseracionem indulgeat

157 Canticles 1:13.

158 Matthew 21:28.

159 Referring to Gratian, *Decretum,* D. 45, cc. 4 and 9; and D. 50, c. 14, in Gratian, *Decretum,* in *Corpus iuris canonici,* part 1, ed. Emil Friedberg (Leipzig 1879; repr. Graz 1959), cols 161, 163–4, and 182–3. But the subsequent text comes from another distinction, see note 163.

160 Read *prelatis* (cf. above note 123); the source has *rectoribus.*

161 Read *temperamentum.*

delinquenti. Ex hiis satis liquet quod nec lenitas mansuetudinis sine seueritate, nec zelus rectitudinis sine mansuetudine in prelatis debet inueniri. Regat ergo discipline rigor mansuetudinem, et mansuetudo ornet sermone[162] rigorem, et sic alterum commendetur ex altero, vt nec districcio sit rigida nec pietas sit remissa. Hec canon.[163]

[k.3] Dicant ergo prelati illud Canticorum 2° capitulo: *Vinea nostra floruit,*[164] scilicet –

per sollicitam in subditis consideracionem, quoad primum;
per piam in necessariis releuacionem, quoad secundum;
et per discretam in corrigendis excessibus reformacionem, quoad tercium.

[k.4] De hac vinea scribitur Mathei 21 capitulo: *Homo erat paterfamilias,* suple Christus, *qui plantauit vineam et sepem circumdedit ei et fodit in ea torcular, et edificauit turrim et locauit eam agricolis.*[165]

Per *sepes*[166] enim intelliguntur officiarii actiui, quibus innuitur[167] vinea ne vulpes rapiant vuas eius, sicut dicitur in primo principali.
Per alteram[168] structuram *turris* intelliguntur claustrales contemplatiui, qui Deum contidie[169] deuotis oracionibus iugiter contemplantur, quoad materiam secundi principalis.
Per *torcular* intelligitur prelatus, vt eius disposicione vue tocius vinee prvdenter calcentur et calcate caucius exprimantur, quoad tercium principalem.

Pro quibus omnibus scribitur Ezechielis 2° capitulo: *Edificabunt domos,* scilicet actiui, *plantabunt vineas,* scilicet prelati, *et habitabunt confidenter,*

---

162 Read *sermonis?*

163 The entire passage from "Ideo circa" on is a selective quotation of Gratian, *Decretum,* Dist. 45, cc. 9–14, in Gratian, *Decretum,* in *Corpus iuris canonici,* part 1, ed. Emil Friedberg (Leipzig 1879; repr. Graz 1959), cols 163–6, with some changes in the wording.

164 Canticles 2:15.

165 Matthew 21:33.

166 Read *sepem?*

167 Read *munitur.*

168 Read *altam.*

169 Read *cotidie.*

scilicet contemplatiui,[170] [f. 250va] hic scilicet cum gracia in presenti et gloria in futuro. **[l]** Quam gloriam ipse nobis concedat qui sine fine viuit et regnat. Amen.

47 Structural Comment

[a] The thema, chosen for the occasion of this sermon, a visitation of a monastic community, here imagined as a vineyard (*vinea*).

[b] For his protheme the preacher has chosen a statement about his own insufficiency, with a supporting authority which is then divided and developed, leading him to

[c] the prayer. This includes first a petition for help in his enterprise (which is verbally linked to the preceding authority and its three members) and then a *commendatio*, a prayer for others, which may have included the dead, benefactors of the monastery, or other persons in authority.

[d] The thema is repeated, and instead of indicating its source again the preacher says "as above."

[f] Instead of a bridge passage the preacher uses an introduction to his thema, in which he explains the three terms of his thema in terms of his visitation.

[g.1] The preacher offers two divisions, first one *intra* (g.1) and then another *extra* (g.2). [g.1] is complex, and its parts are confirmed in [h.1]. The words "Si floruerit" in the second division should be repeated at the beginning of each member; in the scribe's exemplar they probably appeared in front of a large brace ({) spanning the three parts. Apparently the scribe of W had some difficulty with sections [g.1] and [h.1].

[h.1] Confirmation of [g.1]. As just mentioned, the scribe seems to have had some difficulty with his exemplar at this point: the Genesis quotation emerges garbled; the etymology of *Sichem* is cut (according to Jerome *Sychem* means "shoulders," which indicates *opus* or, in later medieval commentaries, *labor corporalis*); and the confirmation of the third part may have dropped out. The (three) confirming authorities are tied together in the final sentence here.

[g.2] The division *extra,* again complex, applies the three terms of the thema to three groups involved in the monastic life and visitation:

170 Ezekiel 28:26.

active monks (i.e., the monastery officials), contemplatives, and prelates (including the visitator). The second division seems to be garbled again, in that the sentence "Et ideo debet florere" fails to mention and distinguish all three social groups. Notice that here the preacher calls his sermon a "collation" (*collacio*), as he already had in [c], and "brief" (*exilis*) – but it is hardly brief, has a full development, and was probably delivered in the morning (see further section 48 below).

[j.1] The development of the three parts (1, 2, 3) begins. Each part starts with a subdivision [i] of the respective member of the main division (g.2), and the members of the subdivision are then developed at paragraph length.

[i.1] A subdivision listing three tasks of active monks, here understood as the monastery officials.

[j.1a] Development of the first task: to take care of worldly business, mainly to protect the monastic community against external enemies here seen in "the boar of the forest" mentioned in Psalm 79:14 alluded to earlier, the "little foxes" of Canticles 2.15, and the "serpents" mentioned by a "philosopher."

[j.1b] Development of the second task: to be good administrators; by means of a simile from nature, biblical figures, and the properties of an object (the palm tree) from another Psalm verse.

[j.1c] Development of the third task: to be fervent in their devotion; again developed with a simile from nature, properties of objects (flower of the field and lily), and yet another biblical authority applied to visitation.

[k.1] The preacher ties up the three points (j.1.a–c) with an authority whose terms are applied to the three requirements to be sought in the officials.

[j.2] Part 2, developing desirable virtues in contemplative monks. Given the careful structure of the entire sermon, the opening of this section is clearly wrong, since it fails to mention "contemplatives." Instead it speaks of *studiositas*, which – according to the later *combinatio partium* at [k.2] – is the third part of the subdivision that one would expect here [i.2], whose three terms would have been the virtues of *obedientia, sanctitas,* and *studiositas.* Further errors occur in the next two paragraphs.

[j.2-a] Development of the first virtue, obedience, by means of a reference to "daily experience," several proof texts, and properties of objects (water lilies and heliotropes).

[j.2-b] Development of the second virtue, saintliness, by means of several proof texts, including biblical commentary.

[j.2-c] Development of the third virtue, studiousness, developed with a reminiscence of how former monks used to copy books, and the properties of an object (lily).

[k.2] *Combinatio* of the points of the missing subdivision [i.2] and their development.

[j.3] Part 3, on prelates (i.e., abbots or priors and visitators).

[i.3] Subdivision of the third member of the main division: three desirable activities in prelates.

[j.3-a] Development of the first activity, care for their monks, including an authority.

[j.3-b] Development of the second activity, providing what is necessary, by means of a proof text and properties of an object (cypress).

[j.3-c] Development of the third activity, discreet correction of failures with a mixture of sternness and mercy, by means of a proof text, here from canon law.

[k.3] *Combinatio* of the three points of part 3.

[k.4] The final tying up (*combinatio*) of parts 1–3 (actually a double one) with authorities whose terms are applied to the three main parts of his sermon ("in primo principali" etc.).

[l] Closing formula with final "Amen."

PART IV

Other Issues

48 *Sermo* vs. *Collatio*

Monastic and university preaching before the fourteenth century knew not only *sermones* but also *collationes*. University regulations as well as extant collections show specifically that the thema of a *sermo* on a given day was taken up again in the afternoon or evening and developed in a *collatio*.[171] To what extent this distinction and practice was observed in the fourteenth and fifteenth centuries, and in different countries, remains an open question – the evidence from actual sermons made during this period in England seems to show that it was not.[172] However, a number of *artes praedicandi* here studied include *collationes* in their discussion and either mention them briefly and synonymously[173] or offer specific formal differences from *sermones*.

The otherwise very long Ars copiosa uses the two terms twice synonymously for the same procedure ("in collationibus ac sermonibus," 14; "in sermone uel collacione," 19) but gives no distinguishing features. Ad erudicionem, however, adds a final section to the material taken from Ars copiosa:

> Finally, we have to speak of the agreement and disagreement between sermons and collations. Thus we say that sermons and collations agree in their general mode of developing and expounding Sacred Scripture.

171 Weijers 1987, pp. 372–8.

172 See Wenzel 2011. The conclusion of my examination was that in actual practice *sermo* and *collatio* were synonymous (243). See also the sample sermon edited and analysed above, in sections 46–7. In light of the distinction between *sermo* and *collatio* described in the following paragraphs, however, it can be said that the anonymous author of the sample sermon was more concerned with building the basic structure of his discourse (i.e., the *forma*) than fleshing it out at greater length (i.e., the *materia*).

173 Thus Ars copiosa.14, 19; Alprão.265, 271. Tuderto likewise uses the two synonymously (1, 81) but specifies that the collation has a preamble (40, see above, p. 25, n. 19). Exercitacio speaks of *collatio* throughout and once uses the two terms synonymously (86vb), but it also says initially that "a collation, as here understood, is a short and complete, duly ordered sermon" (collacio, ut hic accipitur, est sermo breuis et compendiosus debite ordinatus, 85rb) and later (89va–b) declares that in a collation a confirming authority (here called *concordancia*) must not be used in its allegorical sense, which can be done in a sermon (presumably because in the latter the allegorical meaning would be pointed out by the preacher after citing the authority). For other treatises that mention *collatio* see the following discussion.

> Further, they agree that the words *notandum* or *sciendum* are to be used in neither, since these belong to a lecturer [rather than a preacher]. But sermons and collations disagree in their way of beginning and ending. They also disagree in that exclamation, exhortation, and reproach are not to be used in collations. Further, in collations one may use enumeration, but not in sermons. Moreover, in collations virtues must be opposed to vices only in a general way, but in sermons in a specific way. And so forth. (Ad erudicionem.40v)

This difference between the two related treatises – Ars copiosa and Ad erudicionem – suggests that *collatio* received more attention in later – and apparently shorter – *artes*.

In a general way, the collation is characterized as shorter than a sermon. Waleys says: "I do not speak of short collations, in which, after the thema has been divided, two or three authorities are quoted with a short development (*modica pertractatione*), and at once there is the end" (379). Similarly, Exercitacio defines collation as a short sermon and adds that it could also be called *colligatio*, because its members are linked to each other.[174] More telling is the discussion in Piscario. After using the two terms synonymously, its author gives three specific features in which a *collatio* differs from a *sermo*: (1) It has only a brief sentence introducing the thema (such as, "These words speak of the glorious birth ..." 180), whereas the *sermo* can have a longer *introitus*. (2) It must have three members, whereas a *sermo* may have two or four. (3) In it, the members of a division, subdivision, or distinction are to be confirmed (*probari*) but without further exposition, whereas in a *sermo* the confirming authorities may be further defined and developed (180–1).

A peculiar distinction between the two appears in several later *artes*; for instance:

> In everything that has been said, a sermon and a collation are parallel to each other, for a collation is nothing else but the [essential] form of a sermon. For I conceive that there are two things in a sermon, matter and form. "Form" I call a particular way of development, "matter" what underlies the development. (Vade.184)

---

174 "Collacio, ut hic accipitur, est sermo breuis et compendiosus debite ordinatus. Vel potest dici colligacio uel coresponsio, quia in collacione membra sunt ad inuicem colligate" (86va).

The same distinction is made in Hic and Circa. In fact, Hic says that since "a collation must be the subject matter of a sermon ... we must begin with the way and technique of making collations, because what is necessary for a collation is also required for a sermon, but not the reverse" and then devotes its exposition to *collatio* (148–58; cf. Circa.104) before adding a short section on what is special in sermons, namely more than one main division as well as various ways of developing the members of a subdivision (158–60). Similarly, Nota begins with the elements common to both collations and sermons (165v–7) and then adds: "In the following we must briefly see how a collation is expanded into a sermon," namely with several ways of development (*modi dilatandi*; 167). It then gives an example: In dealing with *collatio* earlier, it had taken the thema "He saw and followed him," divided it, and subdivided *saw* into three things that must been seen:

> Our infirmity, to be overcome,
> wordly vanity, to be fled,
> God's goodness, to be desired.

Now it says that in a sermon these three members must be expanded; the first could then appear as follows:

> Our vile infirmity must be overcome for three reasons, because of our birth in sin, our life in misery, and our death in violence. And then authorities from the Bible and the saints must be quoted in support of what the speaker of the collation wants to prove. (167)

It would seem, then, that the difference between the two is that *collatio* has the basic, essential, logical structure of a scholastic sermon (thema – division – subdivision), whereas *sermo* expands the same in different ways, with protheme, introduction, further subdivision, proof texts, and other modes of development. That the sample sermon edited above calls itself *collatio*, thus, agrees with this quite well.

49 Additional Matters

Many, though by no means all, extant sermons written in the late Middle Ages contain an address form, such as *Karissimi*, *Fratres*, *Reverendi*, or longer and exuberant forms like *Studiosissimi magistri, patres atque domini*. Such forms often provide the only hint about what audience the respective sermon was to address, especially whether it was clerical or lay.[175] It is surprising that the *artes* studied for this synthesis do not include any discussion of this element, the *salutatio*, whatsoever.[176] This seems to be a curious omission, especially since some illustrative examples given by the *artes* do use such an address form (for instance, Predicacio.342; Waleys.365, 367; Fecunda.107), and further since the sister art of letter-writing, which was much taught and studied in this time period, concerned itself very much with *salutatio*.[177] It should be noted in this connection that when Eiximenes deals with the prudent behaviour a preacher should maintain, he prescribes that the preacher should never address his audience as "Good people" or "Good sirs" (Eiximenes.317: *Bona gens ... Domini boni*) – advice clearly not followed by English preachers, who regularly used "Good men and women" or "Worshipful sirs."

Yet *artes* often show an awareness that preaching to different audiences, especially to *litterati* or *clerici* as against the common people, may require differences in the sermon structure and material: "One must preach in one way to layfolk, in another to clerics, in one way to city dwellers, in another to people in the country and fields who guard their flocks ... For simple people are better led by similes," and thus a preacher must be especially attentive to in his *introitus sermonis* (Piscario.184; similarly Ars copiosa.16r–v; Borgsleben.69, 71–2; Nota.167v, on dilatation). Negatively, Omnis remarks that "in vernacular sermons to the [common] people" it is not necessary to lay out the parts of a syllogism (268), and that for them it is "very elegant and useful" to cover the four standard topics of Franciscan preaching: vices, virtues, punishment, and glory (272; cf. Higden.56). The most noteworthy formal difference in this respect is that between the two basic forms of the *divisio: intra* against *extra auctoritatem*, where the former is considered to be more appropriate for a clerical, the latter for a lay audience. As was shown in the section on division (section 45-g), the *divisio intra* is

175 See Wenzel 2005a, pp. 9–10.

176 Murphy 1974, p. 338, cites a short *ars* (Caplan 167) with a "salutation to the people"; but his description (seven or eight parts?) and note 96 are suspect.

177 Murphy 1974, pp. 194–268 passim, esp. 205–7; and Camargo 1991. Chobham.261 and Tuderto.38 mention *salutatio* in passing, connecting it with the introductory prayer for grace. This, of course, is the *salutatio angelica*, that is, the "Hail, Mary."

concerned with the words of the thema, while the *divisio extra* uses an idea suggested by it. The very close attention to words and to precise verbal connections that is characteristic of *divisio intra* – which in fact runs through the entire scholastic sermon – makes for a more sophisticated and elegant (*curiosus*) style of preaching, a style which occasionally the writers of *artes* declare less useful for sermons *ad populum.*

Preaching to different audiences naturally calls for differences beyond the structure itself, and the classical discussion of this point by Gregory[178] is often cited or alluded to, though more normally in connection with the preacher's behaviour rather than the form of his sermon (examples at Ashby.27; Chobham.276–7; Higden.13; Eiximenes.315; also Auvergne.196 and 198). One specific device used in the popular preaching of the later Middle Ages is the narrative *exemplum*. It is, says the very popular Thetford, "of great use to layfolk, because, as can be found in Aristotle and Boethius, graphic examples delight them" (multum valet laicis, quoniam sicut habetur tam ab Aristotile quam a Boecio, sensibilibus gaudent exemplis, 92), and then mentions Gregory's *Dialogues*, the *Lives of the Fathers*, and saints' legends as strengthening our good intentions. In this text, the use of *exempla* forms one of several ways to prove a point by reasoning (*ratiocinando*), the others being syllogism, induction, and use of an enthymeme (91–2). The term *exemplum* in the *artes praedicandi* thus includes any example (for a virtue or a vice, for instance) whether it forms a little story or not, and often seems to be no more than a synonym for *similitudo*.[179] Humility, for instance, may be exemplified by a tree, which in order to reach high into the air sends its roots deep into the earth. A frequently found pattern is the triad of *exempla in natura, arte* (human sciences and crafts), and *historia*, the latter comprising figures and events from Scripture, saints' lives, genuine history, but also (Aesopian) fables.[180] Exemplification is therefore

178 Gregory, *Regula pastoralis* 3 (PL 77:49–126), specifies what a preacher should say to audiences differentiated by sex, age, profession, mood, vices, and so on. Another authoritative quotation in this connection is that "*exempla* move more than words." Cf. Gregory, *Dialogi*, prologue (PL 77:153).

179 Thus Waleys speaks of *similitudines* (396–7), whereas Eiximenes calls the same *exempla sensibilia rerum apparencium, animalium, siue aliorum approbata* (322)

180 Thus the longer discussion in Fusignano.80–2; similarly Cordoba.336. In medieval homiletic discourse, *fabula* can refer to any "fabulous" story, from ancient myths to old wives' tales.

treated as one way of development, of expanding the sermon, though it may also be mentioned for use in other parts of the sermon, such as the protheme (to attract attention or frighten the congregation) or the introduction of the thema, wherever some expansion is desired.

What one misses in this regard is the *artes'* more detailed engagement with the kind of narrative *exemplum* that has so much attracted the notice of modern literary scholars, whether for scorn or delight, and evoked some sharp criticism by such medieval moralists as Dante and Chaucer. A quite rare case is the remark that "whenever something concrete is cited for his moral teaching that is to be deduced from it, [the preacher] must take heed that in applying his example he uses proper and carefully chosen words that his subject matter and his example require" (Hic.158). Contemporary pulpit practice is perhaps most closely reflected in Basevorn's discussion, and it is he who states as his view that using more than three narrations in one sermon is bad (Basevorn.314), a view taken over by Higden as "a rule among modern preachers that no more than three *figurae,* three stories, or three exempla be cited in one sermon, so that a principal part does not contain more than one *figura, exemplum,* or narration."[181] Negative remarks about some kinds of *exempla* are not entirely missing: "Also it pleases people more and moves them more to have one division naturally expanded (if it is explained to them according to their capability) than popular trifles and fables" (Eciam ad populum magis placet et magis populum mo[u]et vna diuisio naturaliter prosequta, si eis secundum capacitatem ipsorum exponitur, quam truffe et fabule populares, In predicatore.83rb).

50 Why All This?

Careful application of the teachings that have been surveyed in the preceding sections would have led to a composition of great verbal artistry, with its parts clearly ordered and bound together by means of logical progression and word repetition. Building a house, as it was used in one *ars praedicandi,* is indeed a most fitting simile for the work all their authors envisioned. That preachers in fact employed what the

181 Higden.69. The entire discussion with good illustrations in his chapters 13, 14, and 20 is relevant.

artes taught is witnessed by thousands of surviving sermons from the later Middle Ages, including the sample sermon edited and analysed here in sections 46–7. And occasional contemporary remarks that have had the good fortune of being preserved show that audiences carefully attended to such art, praising a preacher who used it with skill or blaming another who did not.[182]

And yet, to us moderns it all may seem to be an exaggerated concern with structure and form that led to verbal gymnastics, to an empty formality cloaking a quite predictable substance. Did not, on the contrary, St John on Patmos reveal the heart of Christ's message much more powerfully by simply saying, "My children, love one another"? Did not Augustine and Gregory and many others cut much closer to the bone by simply explaining the gospel step by step? And did not, at a later stage, St Francis move his audience by a simple gesture? Why, then, all this concern with *introductio thematis* and *divisio* and *subdivisio* and *processus* and the rest?

Part of an answer is that the scholastic sermon form was the product of new intellectual methods and endeavours that came to blossom in the transition from monastic ideals and forms of mental activity to those at the university. One basic element in this new, scholastic method was the *divisio*. In the words of a modern scholar:

> The scholastic division of the text is an interpretive technique whose idea is rather simple. Starting with the text as a whole, one articulates a principal theme, in the light of which one divides and subdivides the text into increasingly smaller units, often down to the individual words. A scholastic division of the text has at least three essential characteristics. First, the interpreter articulates a theme that provides a conceptual unity to the text and the commentary as a whole. Second, the division penetrates at least to the level of verse; it does not simply articulate large blocks of the text. And third, because the division begins with the whole and then continues through progressive subdivisions, every verse stands in an articulated relation not only with the whole but ultimately with every other part, division, and verse of the text.[183]

182 For some examples see Wenzel 2005b, p. 91.
183 Boyle 2003, p. 276.

What is said here of scholastic *quaestiones*, disputations, and commentaries applies fully to the scholastic sermon, as the preceding pages will have demonstrated. It does not mean that *artes praedicandi* were built like a scholastic *quaestio*, though now and then one may detect a slight smell of the schoolroom.[184] Nor does it mean that, in general, actual sermons followed scholastic structures of argumentation or explored major topics of scholastic theology, though again one may find some slight traces here and there.[185] But it does mean that the student and preacher approached a sacred text, not by meditatively "ruminating" on each word, but by dividing it and pursuing its parts.[186] Both contemplative monks and university scholars pursued the ideal of reaching wisdom, *sapientia*, but – if a pun may be allowed – for monks that lay in savouring (*sapere*) divine truths, whereas the schoolmen fondly declared that "sapientis est ordinare" (the mark of a wise men is to put things in order).[187] And the way in which a biblical scholar and *lector* opened up the sacred text was transferred to the work of preaching. The latter, an activity of formal public speaking, of course required special techniques that properly belonged to the realm of *artes sermocinales*, to rhetoric. To what extent – if at all – classical rhetoric was formally taught in European schools and universities after about 1200 remains a subject of much discussion, and although the blank "Not at all" that may have once been sounded has yielded to more careful and detailed investigations into surviving records and treatises,[188] it is by no means clear how much Cicero's works were actually read and lectured on in that period. As far as the *artes praedicandi* are concerned, their earliest makers, especially Chobham, certainly composed their manuals under the direct guidance of Cicero's *De inventione* and the *Ad Herennium*, but how much such direct influence remained in effect in the fourteenth and fifteenth century remains an open question – in this respect, again,

184 For one such possibility see Wenzel 2008b, pp. 11–13.

185 Particularly by raising an objection and answering it; for some examples, see Wenzel 2005a, pp. 33, 53, 313–16, 381.

186 See the classic study of Leclercq 1962, esp. pp. 14–15 and 76–93. With it one should read the spirited essay by Smith 2000.

187 Aristotle, *Metaphysics* 1.982.a.19, quoted by scholastic theologians, as for instance Aquinas, *Summa theologiae* I.1.6.1. in Thomas Aquinas, *Summa theologiae*, ed. Petrus Caramello, 4 vols (Turin, 1948), 1:5, etc. (What Aristotle actually meant is that the wise man should give orders to others, not receive orders.)

188 For recent findings and surveys, see Ward 1995, Ward 1996, Fredborg 2000, and Camargo 2003.

more surviving *artes* and their interdependence must be studied. In the *artes* that have here been synthesized, "Tullius" is explicitly quoted – besides the obvious Chobham – only in Basevorn (297, 305, 320; also at 248 "in Paradoxis") and in the anonymous Vade (180). Even if one includes a few other occurrences of the term *rhetorica*, one cannot speak of a demonstrable presence of Cicero.[189]

However, what is eminently present is the writers' sense that they are analysing and teaching an art and describing the composition of something appealing and beautiful. Many times they call a particular practice or element not only *artificiosus*, "according to the art (of preaching)," but also *pulcher*, "beautiful,"[190] or they speak of the *decor* and *ornatus* of the sermon. A curious term in this connection is the adjective *curiosus* and its noun *curiositas*. The quality thereby indicated can be blameworthy, but it also – and even in the same text – can evidently have a positive value. The primary witness of this, as it were, semantic duplicity is Basevorn. He speaks of "many things that, in my opinion, belong more to *curiositas* and vanity than to edification" and continues, "So great is human vanity, especially that of the English, that they only care for *curiosa*" (244). But then his treatise is replete with modes and devices that are labelled *curiosa*. In fact, his unique way of calling the main features of a scholatic sermon "ornaments" is justified by his saying that "all these [features], when they occur, adorn the sermon *curiose* and therefore can be called ornaments of the sermon" (249). *Curiosus* must therefore not be translated as "curious" but clearly means something like "elegant." Beside *curiosus* and *ornatus*, the *artes* also speak of *decor*; Quamvis in particular says again and again that "multum foret ad decorem sermonis si ..." (it would enhance the embellishment of the sermon much if ...),[191] and similar statements occur elsewhere.[192]

189 The most noteworthy is Si vis, which uses the phrase *argumentare rethorice* repeatedly together with other verbal reminiscences of Cicero's rhetoric (see above, p. 37). Cordoba makes the general statement that human sciences, including rhetoric, serve the study and exposition of Scripture (346). See also Wenzel 2008a, p. 61. Eiximenes condemns preachers who rely too much on *uerba ... rethorice ornata* (306). The argument for a continuing influence of Cicero has been made by Jennings, most recently in Jennings 2006.

190 Especially Fusignano (passim), but also Waleys (348, 378, 386, 391, etc.), Higden (52, 70), and many others.

191 Quamvis.118, 120, 126.

192 Especially at Alprão.287; Vade.186; Ars copiosa.22, 29. *Decor* is also used, in connection with sermon structure, in Ps.-Bonaventure.10b, 16b; Wales.19v; Fusignano.74; Waleys.370; Hic.152; Nota.165v.

But all these considerations concern the *form* of the sermon. We should not minimize the fact that all medieval *artes praedicandi* were primarily concerned with teaching how to bring the word of God to the people, effectively and for their instruction and moral guidance. In later works of this kind, sermon structure is only the *causa formalis*, while the *causa materialis* is, most succinctly, "the matter to be preached, which is the surpassing doctrine of Christ" (Eiximenes.304).

Works Cited

See also the section "Abbreviations" above, pp. xi–xiii. Biblical references are to the Vulgate edition by Boniface Fischer, Robert Weber, and others, *Biblia Sacra iuxta vulgatam versionem*, 2 vols, third edition (Stuttgart, 1983). Psalms are quoted according to the Hebrew numbering.

Antoninus of Florence. 1480. *Summa Theologica*. Venice: Nicolaus Jenson.

Babcock, June. 1941. "*Ars sermocinandi ac etiam collationes faciendi* of Thomas of Todi, MS Paris, Bibl. Nat. 15965." MA thesis, Cornell University.

Barcelona, Marti de. 1936. OFMCap. "L'Ars Praedicandi de Francesc Eiximenes." In *Homenatge a Antoni Rubió i Lluch: Miscelania d'Estudios Literaris Historicis i Linguisticis*, 2:301–40. Barcelona. Also in *Analecta sacra tarraconensia* 12 (1936):301–40.

Barraque, J.P. 2008. "Les idées politiques de Francesc Eiximenes." *Moyen Age* 114:531–56.

Bériou, Nicole. 1998. *L'avènement des maîtres de la parole: La prédication à Paris au XIIIe siècle.* 2 vols. Collection des Etudes Augustiniennes – Série Moyen Age et Temps Modernes 31. Paris: Institut d'Éudes Augustiniennes.

Bonaventure. 1901. *Doctoris seraphici S. Bonaventurae ... Opera omnia*. Vol. 9. Edited by Patres Collegii a S. Bonaventura. 10 vols in 11. Quaracchi: Collegium s. Bonaventurae, 1882–1902.

Bonner, Stanley F. 1949. *Roman Declamation in the Late Republic and Early Empire*. Liverpool: University Press of Liverpool.

Boyle, John F. 2003. "The Theological Character of the Scholastic 'Division of the Text' with Particular Reference to the Commentaries of Saint Thomas Aquinas." In *With Reverence for the Word: Medieval Scriptural Exegesis in Judaism, Christianity, and Islam*, edited by Jane Dammen McAuliffe, Barry D. Walfish, and Joseph W. Goering, 276–83. Oxford: Oxford University Press.

Boynton, Mary F. 1941. "Simon Alcok on Expanding the Sermon." *Harvard Theological Review* 34:201–16.

Briscoe, Marianne G. 1992. *Artes Praedicandi*. Together with Barbara H. Jaye. *Artes Orandi*. Typologie des sources du moyen âge occidental, fasc. 61. Turnhout: Brepols. Reviewed by Siegfried Wenzel in *Speculum* 69 (1994):1124–6.

Buchwald, S.G. 1921. "Die 'Ars praedicandi' des Erfurter Franziskaners Christian Borgsleben." *Franziskanische Studien* 8:67–74.

Camargo, Martin. 1991. *Ars Dictaminis, Ars Dictandi*. Typologie des sources du moyne âge occidental, fasc. 60. Turnhout: Brepols.

– 2003. "Defining Medieval Rhetoric." In *Rhetoric and Renewal in the Latin West 1100–1540: Essays in Honour of John O. Ward*, edited by Constant J. Mews, Cary J. Nederman, and Rodney M. Thomson. Disputatio 2. Turnhout: Brepols.

– 2010. "How (Not) to Preach: Thomas Waleys and Chaucer's Pardoner." In *Sacred and Profane in Chaucer and Late Medieval Literature: Essays in Honour of John V. FLeming*, edited by Robert Epstein and William Robins, 146–78. Toronto: University of Toronto Press.

Cantini, Gustavo. 1951. "Processus negociandi themata sermonum di Giovanni della Rochelle, OFM." *Antonianum* 26:247–70.

Caplan, Harry. 1925. "A Late Mediaeval Tractate on Preaching." In *Studies in Rhetoric and Public Speaking in Honor of James A. Winans*, edited by A.M. Drummond, 61–90. New York: Century; reprinted in Harry Caplan, *Of Eloquence: Studies in Ancient and Mediaeval Rhetoric*, edited by Anne King and Helen North, 40–79. Ithaca, NY: Cornell University Press, 1970.

– 1929. "The Four Senses of Scriptural Interpretation and the Mediaeval Theory of Preaching." *Speculum* 4:282–90.

– 1933. "'Henry of Hesse' on the Art of Preaching." *PMLA* 48:340–61; reprinted in Harry Caplan, *Of Eloquence: Studies in Ancient and Mediaeval Rhetoric*, edited by Anne King and Helen North, 135–59. Ithaca, NY: Cornell University Press, 1970.

Copeland, Rita, and Ineke Sluiter, eds. 2009. *Medieval Grammar and Rhetoric: Language Arts and Literary Theory, AD 300–1475*. Oxford: Oxford University Press.

D'Alverny, Marie-Therèse, ed. 1965. *Alain de Lille: Texts inédits*. Paris: J. Vrin.

D'Avray, D.L. 1978. "The Wordlists in the *Ars Faciendi Sermones* of Geraldus de Piscario." *Franciscan Studies* 16:184–93.

– 1985. *The Preaching of the Friars: Sermons Diffused from Paris before 1300*. Oxford: Clarendon Press.

De Poorter, A. 1923. "Un manuel de prédication médiévale, le Ms. 97 de Bruges." *Revue Néo-Scolastique de Philosophie* 25:192–205.

Delorme, Ferdinand M. OFM. 1944. "L'*Ars faciendi sermones* de Geraud du Pescher." *Antonianum* 19:169–98.

Donavin, Georgianna. 1997. "'De Sermone Sermonem Fecimus': Alexander of Ashby's *De artificioso modo predicandi.*" *Rhetorica* 15:279–96.

Engelhardt, George J. 1978. "Richard of Thetford: *A Treatise on the Eight Modes of Dilatation.*" *Allegorica* 3:77–160.

Evans, Gillian R., trans. 1981. Alan of Lille, *The Art of Preaching*. Translated by Cistercian Studies Series 23. Kalamazoo, MI: Cistercian Publications.

– 2004. "Gloss or Analysis? A Crisis of Exegetical Method in the Thirteenth Century." In *La Bibbia del XIII Secolo: Storia del testo, storia dell'esegesi. Convegno della Società Internazionale per lo studio del medioevo latino (SISMEL)*, edited by Guiseppe Cremascoli and Francesco Santi, 93–111. Millenno Medioevale 49. Florence: SISMEL.

Evans, Gillian R., and David L. d'Avray. 1980. "An Unusual 'Ars Praedicandi.'" *Medium Aevum* 49:26–31.

Faral, Edmond. 1958. *Les arts poétiques du XIIe et du XIIIe siècle*. Paris: É. Champion.

Fredborg, Karin Margareta. 2000. "Ciceronian Rhetoric and the Schools." In *Learning Institutionalized*, edited by John Van Engen, 21–41. Notre Dame, IN: University of Notre Dame Press.

Gieben, Servus. 1962. "Preaching in the Thirteenth Century: A Note on Ms. Gonville and Caius 439." *Collectanea Franciscana* 32:310–24.

– 1988. "*Rudimentum Doctrinae* di Gilberto di Tournai, con l'edizione del suo Registrum o tavola della materia." In *Bonaventuriana: Miscellanea in Onore de J.-G. Bougerol*, edited by Francisco de Asis Chavero Blanco, 2:621– 80. Bibliotheca Pontifici Athenaei Antoniani 27–8. Rome: Edizioni Antonianum.

Gilson, Etienne. 1932. "Michel Menot et la technique du sermon médiéval." In Gilson, *Les Idees et les Lettres*, 93–154. Paris: J. Vrin.

Goering, Joseph. 2004. "Chobham,Thomas of." ODNB, n.p.

Goldberg, Harriet. 1974. *Jardin de nobles donzellas, Fray Martin de Cordoba: A Critical Edition and Study*. University of North Carolina Studies in the Romance Languages and Literatures 137. Chapel Hill, NC: Department of Romance Languages.

Grosser, Dorothy E., trans. 1949. "Thomas Waleys, *De Modo Componendi Sermones.*" MA thesis, Cornell University.

Gründel, Johannes. 1963. *Die Lehre von den Umständen der menschlichen Handlung*. Beiträge Bäumker 39.5. Münster: Aschendorff.

Hamesse, Jacqueline. 1974. *Les* Auctoritates Aristotelis, *un florilège médiéval: Étude historique et édition critique*. Philosophes Médiévaux 17. Louvain: Publications universitaires.

Hauf, Albert G. 1979. "El 'Ars Praedicandi' de Fr. Alfonso d'Alprão, OFM. Aportacion al Estudio de la Teoria de la Predicacion en la Peninsula Iberica." *Archivum Franciscanum Historicum* 72:233–329.

Hazel, Harry C., Jr. 1972a. "A Translation, with Commentary, of the Bonaventuran 'Ars concionandi.'" PhD dissertation, Washington State University.

– 1972b. "The Bonaventuran 'Ars concionandi.'" *Western Speech* 36:241–50.

– 1973. "The Bonaventuran *Ars concionandi.*" In *S. Bonaventura, 1274–1974,* 2:425–46. Grottaferrata: Collegio S. Bonaventurae.

Henry, Avril. 1990. "'The Pater Noster in a Table Ypeinted' and Some Other Presentations of Doctrine in the Vernon Manuscript." In *Studies in the Vernon Manuscript,* edited by Derek Pearsall, 89–113. Cambridge: D.S. Brewer.

Herbert, J.A. 1910. *Catalogue of Romances in the Department of MSS in the British Museum.* Vol. 3. London: British Museum; reprinted in 1962.

Horner, Patrick J., ed. and trans. 2006. *A Macaronic Sermon Collection from Late Medieval England: Oxford, MS Bodley 649.* PIMS Studies and Texts 153. Toronto: Pontifical Institute of Mediaeval Studies.

Howard, Peter Francis. 1995. *Beyond the Written Word: Preaching and Theology in the Florence of Archbishop Antoninus, 1427–1459.* Florence: Leo S. Olschki.

Humbert de Romanis. 1739. *De eruditione religiosorum praedicatorum.* Edited by Josephus Catalanus. Rome: Antonio de Rubeis.

– 1889. *Opera de vita regulari.* 2 vols. Edited by J.J. Berthier. Rome; reprinted Turin 1956.

– 1951. *Treatise on Preaching.* Translated by Dominican students, Province of St Joseph. Edited by Walter M. Gordon. Westminster, MD: Newman Press.

Jennings, Margaret. 1978. "The Ars Componendi Sermones of Ranulph Higden." In *Medieval Eloquence: Studies in the Theory and Practice of Medieval Rhetoric,* edited by James J. Murphy, 112–26. Berkeley: University of California Press.

– 1989. "*Rhetor Redivivus?* Cicero in the *Artes Praedicandi.*" *Archives d'histoire doctrinale et littéraire du moyen âge,* 91–122.

– 1991. *The Ars Componendi Sermones of Ranulph Higden O.S.B.* Leiden: Brill.

– 2006. "Medieval Thematic Preaching: A Ciceronian Second Coming." In *The Rhetoric of Cicero in Its Medieval and Early Renaissance Commentary Tradition,* edited by Virginia Cox and John O. Ward, 313–34. Brill's Companions to the Christian Tradition 2. Leiden and Boston: Brill.

Jennings, Margaret, and Sally A. Wilson, trans. 2003. Ranulph Higden, *Ars Componendi Sermones.* Paris, Leuven, and Dudley, MA: Peeters.

Johnston, Mark D. 1996. *The Evangelical Rhetoric of Ramon Llull: Lay Learning and Piety in the Christian West around 1300.* New York and Oxford: Oxford University Press.

Kaeppeli, Thomas, OP. 1946. "Eine Prothematasammlung aus Pariser Predigten des 13. Jhdts. in Cod. Vat. Ottob. Lat. 505." In *Miscellanea Giovanni Mercati*, 2:414–30. Studi e testi 121–6. Vatican: Bibliotheca Apostolica Vaticana.

– 1970. *Scriptores Ordinis Praedicatorum Medii Aevi*. 4 vols. Rome: Ad S. Sabinae, 1970–93.

Lausberg, Heinrich. 1969. *Handbuch der literarischen Rhetorik*. 2 vols. Munich: Max Hueber.

Lawler, Traugott, ed. 1974. John of Garland, *Parisiana Poetria*. New Haven: Yale University Press.

Leclercq, Jean. 1961. OSB. *The Love of Learning and the Desire for God: A Study of Monastic Culture*. Translated by Catharine Misrahi. New York: New American Library.

Lull, Raymond. 1961. *Liber de praedicatione*. Edited by Abraham Soria Flores, OFM. In *Raimundi Lulli Opera latina*, edited by Fridericus Stegmüller. Palma: Maioricensis Schola Lullistica.

Miller, Joseph M. 1969. "Guibert de Nogent's *Liber quo ordine sermo fieri debeat*: A Translation of the Earliest Modern Speech Textbook." *Today's Speech* 17: 45–56.

Minnis, A.J., and A.B. Scott. 1988. *Medieval Literary Theory and Criticism c. 1100–c. 1375: The Commentary-Tradition*. Oxford: Clarendon Press.

Morenzoni, Franco, ed. 1988. Thomas de Chobham, *Summa de Arte Praedicandi*. Corpus Christianorum Continuatio Mediaevalis 82. Turnhout: Brepols.

– 1991. "Aux origines des *Artes Praedicandi*: Le *De artificioso modo predicandi* d'Alexandre d'Ashby." *Studi Medievali*, 3rd series, anno 32, fasc. 2:887–935.

– 1995. "La littérature des *artes praedicandi* de la fin du XIIe au début du XVe siècle." In *Sprachtheorien in Spätantike und Mittelalter*, edited by Sten Ebbesen, 339–59. Geschichte der Sprachtheorie 3. Tübingen: Gunter Narr Verlag.

– 1997. "Parole du prédicateur et inspiration divine d'après les Artes Praedicandi." In *La Parole du prédicateur, V–XV siècles*, edited by Rosa Maria Dessi and Michel Lauwers, 271–90. Nice: Z'éditions.

– 2005. "*Predicatio est rei predicate humanis mentibus presentatio*: le sermon pour la Dédicace de l'église de Guillaume d'Auvergne." In *Autour de Guillaume d'Auvergne (+ 1249)*, edited by F. Morenzoni and J.-Y. Tilliette, 292–322. Turnhout: Brepols.

– 2006. "A propos d'une *ars praedicandi* attribuée à Nicole Oresme." *Archivum Franciscanum Historicum* 99: 251–81.

Morenzoni, Franco, and Thomas H. Bestul, eds. 2004. Alexander Essebiensis, *Opera theologica*. Vol. 1, *De artificioso modo praedicandi, Sermones*. Corpus Christianorum Continuatio Medievalis 138. Turnhout: Brepols.

Murphy, James J., ed. 1971. *Three Medieval Rhetorical Arts*. Berkeley; reissued Tempe, AZ: Arizona Center for Medieval and Renaissance Studies, 2001.

– 1974. *Rhetoric in the Middle Ages: A History of Rhetorical Theory from Saint Augustine to the Renaissance*. Berkeley, Los Angeles, and London: University of California Press.

Ps.-Aquinas. 1483. *Modus predicandi*. Memmingen: Albrecht Kunne. This and other incunable editions are available scanned at http://tudigit.ulb.tu-darmstadt.de.

Rex, Richard. 2004. "Alcock, Simon." ODNB, n.p.

Rivers, Kimberly A. 1999. "Memory and Medieval Preaching: Mnemonic Advice in the *Ars Praedicandi* of Francesc Eiximenes (ca. 1327–1409)." *Viator* 30:252–84.

– 2010. *Preaching the Memory of Virtue and Vices: Memory, Images, and Preaching in the Later Middle Ages*. Sermo 4. Turnhout: Brepols.

Ross, Woodburn O. 1937. "A Brief Forma Praedicandi." *Modern Philology* 34:337–44.

– ed. 1940. *Middle English Sermons Edited from British Museum MS Royal 18.B.xxiii*. Early English Text Society, original series, 209. London: Oxford University Press.

Roth, Dorothea. 1956. *Die mittelalterliche Predigttheorie und das "Manuale Curatorum" des Johann Ulrich Surgant*. Basler Beiträge zur Geschichtswissenschaft 158. Basel: Helbing und Lichtenhahn.

Rubió, Fernando, OSA. 1959. "*Ars Praedicandi* de Fray Martin de Cordoba." *La Ciudad de Dios* 172:327–48.

Schneyer, Johannes Baptist. *Die Unterweisung der Gemeinde über die Predigt bei scholastischen Predigern. Eine Homiletik aus scholastischen Prothemen*. Veröffentlichungen des Grabmann-Institutes, Neue Folge, 4. Munich: Schöningh.

Smith, Lesley. 2000. "The Use of Scripture in Teaching at the Medieval University." In *Learning Institutionalized: Teaching in the Medieval University*, edited by John Van Engen, 229–43. Notre Dame: University of Notre Dame Press.

Swanson, Jenny. 1989. *John of Wales: A Study of the Works and Ideas of a Thirteenth-Century Friar*. Cambridge: Cambridge University Press.

– 2004. "Wales, John of." ODNB, n.p.

Taylor, John. 2004. "Higden, Ranulf." ODNB, n.p.

Tugwell, Simon, ed. 1982. *Early Dominicans: Selected Writings*. Classics of Western Spirituality. New York: Paulist Press.

– 1989. "Humbert of Romans's Material for Preachers." In *De Ore Domini: Preacher and Word in the Middle Ages*, edited by Thomas L. Amos, Eugene A. Green, and B. Kienzle, 105–17. Kalamazoo, MI: Medieval Institute Publications.

– 1993. "De huiusmodi sermonibus texitur omnis recta predicatio: Changing Attitudes towards the Word of God." In *De l'homélie au sermon: Histoire de la prédication médiévale*, edited by Jacqueline Hamesse and Xavier Hermand, 159–68. Actes du Colloque International de Louvain-la-Neuve (9–11 juillet 1992). Louvain-la-Neuve: Université Catholique de Louvain.

– 2004. "Waleys, Thomas." ODNB, n.p.

Ward, John O. 1995. *Ciceronian Rhetoric in Treatise, Scholion and Commentary.* Typologie des sources du moyen âge occidental 58. Turnhout: Brepols.

– 1996. "Rhetoric in the Faculty of Arts at the University of Paris and Oxford in the Middle Ages: A Summary of the Evidence." *Bulletin Du Cange* 54:158–231.

Weijers, Olga. 1987. *Terminologie des universités au XIIIe siècle.* Lessico Intellettuale Europeo 39. Rome: Edizioni dell' Ateneo.

Wenzel, Siegfried. 1976. "Chaucer and the Language of Contemporary Preaching." *Studies in Philology* 73:138–61; reprinted in Siegfried Wenzel, *Elucidations: Medieval Poetry and Its Religious Backgrounds*, 139–60. Louvain, Paris, and Walpole, MA: Peeters, 2010.

– 1985. "Poets, Preachers, and the Plight of Literary Critics." *Speculum* 60:343–63; reprinted in *Elucidations*, 213–41.

– 1986. *Preachers, Poets, and the Early English Lyric*. Princeton, NJ: Princeton University Press.

– 1994. *Macaronic Sermons: Bilingualism and Preaching in Late-Medieval England.* Ann Arbor, MI: University of Michigan Press.

– 1995. "A Sermon Repertory from Cambridge University." *History of Universities* 14 (1995–6):43–67.

– 2005a. *Latin Sermon Collections from Later Medieval England: Orthodox Preaching in the Age of Wyclif.* Cambridge: Cambridge University Press.

– 2005b. "The Arts of Preaching." In *The Cambridge History of Literary Criticism.* Vol. 2, *The Middle Ages*, edited by Alastair Minnis and Ian Johnson, 84–96. Cambridge: Cambridge University Press.

– 2008a. "A Dominican (?) *Ars Praedicandi* in Sermon Form." *Archivum Fratrum Praedicatorum* 78:51–78.

– trans. 2008b. *Preaching in the Age of Chaucer: Selected Sermons in Translation.* Washington, DC: The Catholic University of America Press.

– 2011. "A Note on *Collatio* in Late-Medieval Preaching." In *Swedish Students at the University of Vienna in the Middle Ages*, edited by Olle Ferm and Erika Kihlman, 235–43. Stockholm: Centre for Medieval Studies, Stockholm University.

– 2013a. "The Appearance of *Artes praedicandi* in Medieval Manuscripts." In *Medieval Manuscript Miscellanies: Composition, Authorship, Use*, edited by

Lucie Doležalová and Kimberley Rivers, 102–11. Medium Aevum Quotidianum, Sonderband 31. Krems: Medium Aevum Quotidianum, 2013.

– 2013b. *The Art of Preaching: Five Medieval Texts and Translations.* Washington, DC: The Catholic University of America Press.

Zafarana, Zelina. 1981. "La predicazione francescana." In *Francescanesimo e Vita Religiosa dei Laici nel '200.* Convegno della Società Internazionale di Studi Francescani, Assisi, 16–18 ottobre 1980, 203–50. Assisi: Università degli studi de Perugia. Reprinted in Zelina Zafarana, *Da Gregorio VII a Bernardino da Siena: Saggi de storia medievale,* edited by O. Capitani et al., 141–86. Todi: La Nuova Italia Editrice, 1987.

Zumkeller, Adolar, OSA. 1970. "Unbekannte Konstanzer Konzilspredigten der Augustiner-Theologen Gottfried Shale und Dietrich Vrie." *Analecta Augustiniana* 33:5–74.

Index

Topics mentioned in the text by either their Latin or their English name are here indexed under the English word only, except for specific technical terms (such as *manuductio*).

www.ingramcontent.com/pod-product-compliance
Lightning Source LLC
LaVergne TN
LVHW090200080826
844660LV00013B/887/J

* 9 7 8 1 4 4 2 6 5 0 1 0 7 *